American POWs of World War II

American POWs of World War II

Forgotten Men Tell Their Stories

TOM BIRD

Westport, Connecticut
London

Library of Congress Cataloging-in-Publication Data

Bird, Tom, 1956–
    American POWs of World War II : forgotten men tell their stories /
    Tom Bird.
        p.   cm.
    Includes bibliographical references (p.   ) and index.
    ISBN 0-275-93707-0
    1. World War, 1939–1945—Prisoners and prisons. 2. World War,
    1939–1945—Personal narratives, American. 3. World War, 1939–1945—
    Psychological aspects. 4. Prisoners of war—United States—
    Biography. 5. Prisoners of war—United States—Psychology.
    I. Title.
    D805.A2B57   1992
    940.54′72′0922—dc20   91-46991

British Library Cataloguing in Publication Data is available.

Library of Congress Catalog Card Number: 91-46991
ISBN: 0-275-93707-0

First published in 1992

Praeger Publishers, 88 Post Road West, Westport, CT 06881
An imprint of Greenwood Publishing Group, Inc.

Printed in the United States of America

The paper used in this book complies with the
Permanent Paper Standard issued by the National
Information Standards Organization (Z39.48–1984).

10 9 8 7 6 5 4 3 2 1

To Barbara Ann Bird,
my wife,
my best friend,
my forever partner

Contents

Part Three: The Jewish POW

Preface

I chose to write this book on the experience of the World War II American prisoners of war for several reasons. First, I felt that their tales had never been fully documented before. Second, I chose this topic because these men were also the first POWs in the automated age of war, which made the severity of the conditions that they were asked to endure so much more extreme, confusing, and penetrating. Not only were their captors totally unprepared for their numbers, but we, as a country and as a people, were inadequately equipped as well to deal with them when they were liberated and after they returned home. Thus the World War II POWs were never recognized for the unique consequences of their captivity until 35 years after their release.

Last, I chose this subject because I felt that within the stories of these men's trials there is a message for us all. I felt that their tales of incarceration and survival were dramatic reflections of what the average human being, whether recognized or not, deals with on an everyday basis. For as former POW Tom Grove says, "We are all incarcerated in one way or another." How we deal with that incarceration and its results determines what type of life we will lead. That point is more fully dealt with in Dr. Charles Stenger's papers and interview that follow.

The men whose stories are chronicled in this book were chosen for the candor and depth with which they convey their tales. In an effort to retain as much of their heartfelt recollections as possible, editing of their interviews was held to a minimum.

I hope that readers will receive as much from this book as I did from writing it.

Acknowledgments

This book could never have been completed without the undying effort of several committed and unselfish individuals.

I would like to thank my editor, Dan Eades, for his God-like patience; Rick Canevin, of the Veteran's Hospital in Pittsburgh, Pennsylvania, for his work and inspiration; Chuck Williams and Sally Morgan from the National Association for American POWs for their time, their insight, their referrals, and their overall assistance. As well, I would like to offer my heartfelt thanks to those former POWs who offered me their time and assistance but whose stories I was unable to fit into the enclosed.

Last, I want to acknowledge the efforts of my transcriptionist Trish Taylor, and especially of my typist, friend, student, and the future author Cindi Palotas, without whose devoted efforts this book would have likely never been completed.

INTRODUCTION TO THE POW EXPERIENCE

A Look at the Inhospitable World of the Hostage and Prisoner of War and Its Impact on Their Lives

Charles A. Stenger

In today's uneasy and uncertain world, we cannot dismiss as entirely unrealistic the possibility that we or some member of our families may suddenly find ourselves under the complete control of an individual or individuals acting ruthlessly either in their own self-interest or in the name of some cause. Indeed, such events appear to be occurring with rapidly increasing frequency both in this country and abroad. The Iranian hostage situation, which held the attention of much of the world for more than a year, is a dramatic example of the power such events can have on victims and non-victims alike.

An understanding and appreciation of what it means to be in a situation in which your life is in jeopardy or your most private rights as a human being are violated is essential if survivors are to be helped and potential victims prepared for such an ordeal.

How does one adjust to and endure such an experience, and what will be the long-term physical and psychological consequences? To help answer this question, there is a considerable body of research on survivors of concentration camps, prisoner-of-war stockades and hostages held as individuals or groups under a wide variety of circumstances. There is general consistency of findings and widespread agreement among experts concerning the major universal consequences. There is also extensive laboratory research on animals and humans directly relevant to the question. Last, there are

This chapter was developed by the author from an address to the Division of Psychologists in Public Service at the American Psychological Association Convention in Montreal, Canada, on September 2, 1980, and was rewritten and updated in February 1981.

thousands of first-hand accounts by survivors that provide considerable insight into the traumatic nature of these experiences and their consequences.

Circumstances under which civilians are taken hostage and those in which military personnel are taken prisoner during combat seem worlds apart. The U.S. ambassador to Colombia, Diego Asencio, was attending a social function at the Dominican Embassy in Bogota when it was taken over by force in a burst of gunfire. Richard Queen and other members of the staff left the U.S. Embassy in Iran by a side door when the furor began. They at first perceived it as simply a more extreme expression of the daily protests staged in front of the building by Iranian nationals. "I was lolligagging along and turned down the wrong street," Queen said. "We thought we were going to Dick's house to sit it out and play bridge. . . . We just sort of ambled along and they took us."

He was released due to illness more than eight months later. His 52 colleagues were to remain much longer. In March 1977, in Washington, D.C., the Hanafi Muslims took over the B'nai B'rith headquarters, the National Islamic Center, and part of the District of Columbia Municipal Building. Those taken hostage—more than 100—were simply engaged in routine daily activities at the time they were captured. In contrast, military personnel are involved in destructive actions designed to kill or injure the enemy. They are under acute tension and experience an extreme sense of danger. The possibility of coming under the complete control of the enemy, who is also trying to destroy them, is usually seen as remote as well as highly undesirable. When the event actually occurs, the military person, as with civilians taken hostage in circumstances described earlier, experiences it as sudden, unexpected, and traumatic.

The difference in the sequence of events prior to captivity rapidly fades in significance in the face of the common psychological experiences they now share. The following description by an American captured during the Vietnam War will illustrate:

Almost from the moment of capture you have two devastating feelings. One, that it's the end of the world, that you have lost and will never again be part of that world to which you really felt you belonged and counted for something. Second, an intense fear of death that never leaves you. You see your capturers as totally omnipotent and yourself as totally helpless. You know that any threat from him is a *promise* that could happen right now and you dare not challenge anything. Your confidence goes downhill radically almost immediately.[1]

Similarly, when Richard Queen was asked during a press conference whether he felt his life was in danger, he replied, with obvious emotion, "You know, in a situation like that, the imagination does horrible things, and I really don't want to go much further into that."

Ambassador Diego Asencio was able to talk about his experiences more easily, describing the almost immediate sense of helplessness, passivity, and resignation that developed in many of his fellow hostages and emphasizing that he didn't doubt for a second they would be killed if their captors believed it suited their purposes.

It is clear that, regardless of the circumstances, the initial impact is devastating and profound for all. Victims are flooded with the following reactions: a strong feeling of unreality (this can't be really happening); an extreme sense of danger; a sense of total vulnerability; a deep feeling of helplessness; and an intense feeling of defenselessness and powerlessness to fight or flee. The captors are perceived as exceedingly powerful, hostile, threatening, and unpredictable. This is continuously experienced on a moment-to-moment basis with the captors ever-present physically or psychologically. Both civilian and military hostages see themselves as pawns for any reasons that serve the purpose of their captors. While it is true that many more military personnel than civilian hostages are killed or beaten soon after capture, all feel the same pervasive sense of danger and uncertainty. The acute sense of danger and vulnerability are readily recognized reactions. However, on a basic personality level, a more insidious, highly destructive psychological process occurs. Termed "idiocide" by philosopher Paul Weiss, it means the "killing" of the individual as a unique, integrated human being.[2] He asserts that the process occurs no matter why the person was taken prisoner or hostage.

Primarily, individuals experience a deep sense of loss or disconnection from the world they knew and believed, and lose a sense of worth to themselves and others. In that world they fulfilled many functions, many roles, that repeatedly verified their value and worth. Self-esteem and self-confidence nurtured and strengthened through repetition of these roles erode in the hostage situation. This occurs because opportunities to actively engage in psychologically self-reinforcing acts diminish greatly or disappear completely. Individuals are confronted with situations in which they are unable to cope in an active way. Instead, complete submission and compliance are required. Their world becomes indifferent to their needs and is almost totally unresponsive to them as unique individuals. The situation is not unlike that of laboratory rats that are treated as interchangeable with each other and utilized in a wholly arbitrary manner for any purpose desired by their owners. Hostages of all kinds feel that they are considered as little more than objects, that they have no value as individuals, and are expendable.

The devastating effect of being treated as an object can be better understood in terms of its contrast with the learning process that begins in early childhood and is well established by adulthood. This process teaches children that they can be essentially in control of their own lives.

The world is manageable if one develops the skills and takes the time and effort to master or influence it. We equate the concept of maturity with the ability to "take charge of one's life" in a controlled, responsible manner. The countless repetitions of developed patterns of response from simple habits to self-directed activities concerning the next minute, next hour, or next day all reaffirm for the individual that he can cope effectively and therefore has value to himself and others. A critical part of this is in planning for and predicting the future. Research with young children show that they resist parental figures who try to deviate from known endings of familiar bedtime stories. The child is reassured by predicting what will occur next in the story and reacts adversely to loss of such "control." This ability to "control" the future is totally absent in the hostage situation, even in planning for the most routine aspects of everyday life.

The occurrence of hundreds of events in which self-esteem and self-confidence are eroded, the sense of loss concerning a world that was meaningful, and an acute awareness of the stark realities of the immediate captive world greatly reduce the feelings of hope and sense of purpose in life for many hostages. The response of resignation and helplessness described by Ambassador Asencio has been demonstrated in research on wild rats by Curt Richter (1957) at Johns Hopkins University over 25 years ago.[3]

The rats were placed in a small metal cage. A sliding door was opened and the rat would see a dark opening (a black opaque bag). The rat would shoot through the opening, its escape immediately cut off. The rat would then be gently pushed toward the end of the bag and simply held, through the walls of the bag, in the hand of the experimenter. Over 2,000 rats were held in this way and, despite their fierce and aggressive nature, none ever made an attempt to bite the experimenter through the bag. Many died simply from this restraint. Those that did not were placed in a large glass cylinder filled with water and forced to sink or swim. All died promptly on immersion, in contrast to usual laboratory rats under the same circumstances. Electrocardiographic records were taken during this second phase and, contrary to the usual response to stress of acceleration in heart rate, rats succumbing promptly had an immediate slowing of the heart rate. The researchers concluded that when fight or flight are not available, hopelessness and resignation follow with major psychophysiological responses that adversely affect survival.

In this experiment, it was found that if wild rats were repeatedly held for just a few seconds and then released from this state, or if immersed in the cylinder of water very briefly and then "rescued," they showed no signs of giving up during later immersion. Instead, they continued to swim as long as domestic rats. A subsequent study by Wittrig, Mehl, and Deter (1965) with laboratory rats revealed that rats subjected to various kinds of stress in early life swam more than twice as long as a control group in which no stress was present during the same period of time.[4] Both experimenters hypothesized that rats, wild or domestic, that are permitted to survive an overwhelming situation develop an "immunity" to the "hopelessness" response.

In hostage situations, the ability of the captive to retain hope, regardless of the inhumane conditions being experienced, can be the crucial factor in survival. This hope can be rooted in many things. Religious beliefs, being a part of a close family situation as a child or adult, feeling a strong sense of group with fellow hostages, deep feelings of patriotism, and a "righteous" cause are all examples repeatedly stated by hostages. In each of these examples, the individuals find strength to cope in sources outside of themselves, balancing their own diminished coping skills and eroding self-esteem. A poignant account of one American soldier, Theodore Gostas, who spent more than five years as a prisoner in Vietnam, is simply called "Prisoner" and was written while he was there.[5] It provides a vivid picture of his daily struggles to retain a reason to live. Several excerpts follows:

Beauty is a catharsis for pain. These rivers are beautiful, these mountains, these trees. Even the leeches are beautiful to other leeches. At least we eat, and sleep! But why this pain again? I see! The guards have fed us and made us to lie down and sleep in an ant pile! The pain of the ants is greater than their beauty. I was wrong—no beauty is greater than this pain.

My wife! My love! Our lips kiss so often and now they have tied my hands behind my back and have said you shall die, you shall never see your wife again! No! I shout, hell or heaven, earth or sea, we shall kiss each other's lips again, again, again.

Hostages also strive to reduce hopelessness and a diminished sense of self by retaining as many of their previous roles while in captivity as possible regardless of the degree of modification necessary. That is, they continue to consider themselves as a leader with important responsibilities, continue to act as a soldier, or function as a doctor or medic where possible. Their aim was to do or think about doing those things in which they could still experience themselves as coping successfully, regardless of how insignificant those actions might be. Repeatedly and slowly folding objects of clothing as neatly and perfectly as possible is a common device by which hostages try to prove to themselves they can meet a "challenge." Hostages find that ruminating on the separation from one's family or loved ones, in contrast to reminiscing about pleasant activities involving them, intensified the sense of pain and hopelessness. Most learn not to allow themselves this reaction.

It is not uncommon for hostages individually or in groups to risk injury or punishment by challenging the captors, exceeding limits of freedom set for them within the captive situation or humiliating their captors in some way. Such actions are desperate ego-building efforts rather than a serious attempt to challenge the captor's power and control. In this sense, they are similar to children who test the limits of parental authority and seek greater individual attention and recognition. "If I can make you angry or force you to react to me, then I must count" is the concept being expressed.

In a very different way, the hostage may seek to reduce the sense of threat and increase the feeling of counting as an individual by identification with the captors (as may have occurred with Patty Hearst) or by seeing them as benevolent and worthwhile rather than dangerous and indifferent. The latter has come to be called the "Stockholm syndrome" after the response of hostages in a bank holdup. The hostage, in this psychologically traumatic state, sees the captor as "good guys," in the words of Martin Symonds (1980). This perception stems from the realization that the captor who could kill them is, in fact, choosing not to do so. Symonds notes that during negotiation for release, the captor is seen as the protector who wants to free the prisoner, while those negotiating for their release are perceived as rejecting, indifferent, and—by failing to comply with the captor's demands—jeopardizing their lives.[6] This identification with the captor often continues after release and it is unusual for hostages to condemn or hate their captors after release. The experience was too intense for the hostage to feel that someone who had such complete power over them can later be weak and non-threatening. Symonds cautions would-be rescuers not to make plans for escape based on the cooperation of the captives. He states, "They must remember that to victims of terror an open door is not perceived as an open door." Patty Hearst's participation in a bank robbery with her captors is believed by many experts in hostage behavior to be an extreme example of this kind of psychological response.

From the above discussion, it is abundantly clear that it is almost impossible to overstate the enormity of the impact of being a hostage, whether civilian or military. The individual is driven by extreme and persistent danger and by the erosion of self-esteem and self-confidence to desperate psychological measures to retain hope for the future and to survive until that day comes. Tragically, once it arrives, the victim is not free from its deep emotional impact reinforced so frequently and intensively that it is indelibly stamped on the personality.

Eitinger refers to the long-term impact in these words: "Whether the person realizes it or not the limited sentence in captivity has become a life sentence."[7] The danger to the hostage after release is what Symonds calls the "second injury," caused by would-be helpers, family, friends, or professionals who treat the episode as finished and fail to respond to the intense basic need of nurturing comfort to reverse the idiocide process and to rebuild the damaged sense of self. Prevention of further damage requires deep appreciation of the stressful and dehumanizing process to which the victim was exposed. It involves recognizing that the individual made necessary adjustments to an extremely pathological situation and that these involved sacrificing previous life-adaptation patterns and damaged the sense of self. Reintegration can occur over time but it does not occur simply because the hostage episode has ended. The usual insistence on the part of many hostages that they are all right psychologically cannot be accepted at face value. It reflects both a continuation of the "survival" mentality and a "flight to health" in an effort to put the traumatic experience in the past.

The many studies of prisoners of war and the few studies of civilian hostage victims all show that anxiety reactions of all kinds are the most critical readjustment problem. These stress reactions occur regardless of the length of time in captivity. They occur with much greater frequency than in individuals who may have experienced great stress, such as combat veterans, but did not experience the helplessness, vulnerability, and diminished sense of self as did the hostage.

Veterans Administration studies show that the incidence of anxiety neurosis among the 75,000 veterans who had been prisoners of war in Germany during World War II was significantly higher than among other World War II veterans with service-related disabilities.[8] It ranged from 22 percent for those held prisoner for less than three months to 37 percent of those confined more than two years. In contrast, only 11 percent of the veterans who had not been prisoners of war were service-connected for anxiety reactions. A similar disparity occurs among prisoners of the Japanese in World War II or of the North Koreans in the Korean War. The significance of this becomes even greater because, as the longitudinal studies of former prisoners of war conducted by the National Academy of Sciences show, prisoners of war had at least twice the incidence of anxiety neurosis of carefully matched combat control groups. The actual incidence of anxiety neurosis is probably much higher than the Veterans Administration data show since many POWs, due to absence of medical records during confinement or when first repatriated, have been unable to "prove" the relationship of this anxiety to their captivity, particularly when the onset was delayed.

A study by Rona Fields (1980) of 12 hostages held three days in the Hanafi muslim take-over of the B'nai B'rith headquarters showed that within one year, none had sought professional mental health services.[9] Most of them initially denied any ill effects from the hostage experience.

The National Academy of Sciences has conducted both mortality and morbidity longitudinal studies of World War II and Korean War prisoners. In all cases, the controls were combat veterans serving in the same theater of operations. The mortality data through 1975 show that a leading cause of death for POWs is trauma involving accidents, suicides, or homicides.

Robert J. Keehan, who carried out an analysis in 1980, said that the high incidence of death from trauma could reflect failures of former prisoners of war to resolve anxiety, the diminished sense of status, or the reduced sense of meaning or direction in life developed in the captive experience.[10]

While there is general acceptance of the effects of stress on physiological processes, controversy remains as to how this operates in regard to specific body systems. Hans Selye (1976) has defined stress as the non-specific response of the body to any demand in terms of the somatic changes that occur. He postulates a "general adaptation syndrome" that is characterized by three possible phases: alarm, resistance, and exhaustion. He states:

A certain amount of stress is needed. . . . [O]n the other hand we must learn the limits of our endurance before we exceed them dangerously. . . . [E]xposure to stress leaves an indelible scar. It uses up an adaptability reservoir that cannot be replaced.[11]

A study was done by Richard Rahe (1964) concerning the possible effects of ordinary life-change events on 2,500 sailors who were going to sea for six months.[12] A questionnaire was used to identify the frequency and type of changes such as moving, changing duty assignments, marriage, divorce, and so on occurring over the preceding six months. Those with the highest number of changes were called a high-risk group and those with the fewest, a low risk group. During the first month at sea, the high-risk group had 90 percent more illnesses of all types than did the low-risk group. This dropped to 30 percent the second month and remained constant throughout the following four months. However, when both new and recurring illnesses were considered, together with their severity, the high-risk group exceeded the low-risk group for every one of the six months.

When severe stress such as that faced by those in concentration camps or prisoner of war camps is experienced, the adverse effects on the body are more evident. Studies done in Canada, Norway, Denmark, Poland, Bulgaria, Germany, France, Japan, Israel, and the United States all show long-range adverse effects on health. The following excerpt from an article by Segal, Hunter, and Segal (1976), "Universal Consequences of Captivity," presents the situation as follows:

The underlying hypothesis is that captivity makes an impact on health and behavior which is relatively constant across nations and cultures, that the physical, psychological, and social costs of incarceration experiences are to some extent predictable no matter who finds himself in the role of the captor and captive. The aim here is to *underscore* the *consistency* with which captivity effects appear across time and across widely *divergent settings* and populations of POWS. . . .

The environment of captivity typically contains a potent blend of physical hardship and privation on the one hand and enormous psychological stress and trauma on the other. . . . [It] is clear in any case that survivors . . . are at risk for a staggering range of physical disabilities and symptoms that can be ascribed to the over-all captivity episode.[13] [emphasis added]

The NAS longitudinal studies of morbidity in former POWs were last reported by Gilbert Beebe (1975) on data through 1967.[14] He notes that his findings may underestimate differences between POWs and combat controls because survival through the period of confinement (approximately 40 percent of prisoners died in Asian camps in World War II and Korea) probably depended heavily on superior physical constitution and emotional maturity. His data show that former prisoners of war, particularly those of Asian countries, have a higher incidence of a wide range of diseases, emotional and physical, that do their matched controls. They are admitted to hospitals more frequently and remain as patients longer. Psychiatric conditions are the most common problem among all POWs, but nutritional disorders, neuritis, peripheral nerve damage, eye disorders, intestinal disorders, liver and genito-urinary disorders, heart disease, and diseases of bones and movement are higher for prisoners in Japan and Korea.

The Veterans Administration study completed in June 1980 shows that more than fifty percent of those held prisoner in Japan and 41 percent of those held prisoner in Germany during World War II are "service-connected" for their disability, as compared with 9.6 percent of all World War II veterans. For Korean War veterans, 59 percent of the POWs are service-connected, as compared with 5 percent of the Korean veterans as a whole. As pointed out earlier, these differences might be even greater since the medical records on which service connection is based are unfortunately lacking or inadequate for most POWs.

Despite the conclusive evidence concerning the long-range adverse consequences of deprivation, stress, and dehumanization on subsequent physical health and psychological adjustment in hundreds of studies conducted in this country and abroad, the full story may not yet be known. The fact that there is often a delay in the emergence of many medical conditions caused by nutritional deficiencies makes it extremely difficult to differentiate them from causal factors unrelated to the hostage experience. Similarly, the impact of extreme and prolonged stress on the future capacity of the body to resist disease processes, particularly those associated with aging, is not yet understood. Anecdotal accounts that those subjected to severe stress do suffer such consequences are extremely common and convincing.

Psychologists and other mental health professionals can provide an important public service through their professional associations as well as individually. They can do so by urging responsible officials to conduct thorough medical and psychological examinations and offer preventive follow-up care to victims and their families. Rape victims, who experience many of the immediate and long-range consequences described in this book, are increasingly being provided both immediate and follow-up psychological assistance and support. The Americans who were held hostage in Iran for 444 days could be the first real beneficiaries of a cooperative response from professional associations. A group of 11 experts, the Hostage and Family Adjustment Committee, is now working with the joint support of the American Psychiatric Association and American Psychological Association. These professionals bring considerable expertise to the committee through their previous experience with prisoners of war, the Jonestown crisis, the Hanafi Muslim incident, Chowchilla school bus kidnapping, and other hostage situations. The purpose of the committee is to offer consultation and support to professionals working with the hostages and their families either under the auspices of the State Department or on a private basis.

"Happy endings" for survivors of all types of hostage situations will occur, not simply because they were released, but because they were assisted through the complex psychological readjustment process that follows by family members, friends, and professionals who understood what they have been through and responded sensitively and appropriately.

NOTES

1. Weiss, Paul. Idiocide. *Evaluation and Change*, special issue, 1980.
2. Ibid.
3. Richter, Curt P. On the Phenomenon of Sudden Death in Animals and Men, *Psychosomatic Medicine*, 19 (3): 1957.
4. Wittrig, John, Mary M. Mehl, and Francis H. Deter. Developmental Stress, Emotionality and Survival: A New Test. *Proceedings of the American Psychological Association*, 1: 1965.
5. Gostas, Theodore W. *Prisoner*. New York: Western Publishing, 1974.
6. Symonds, Martin. The "Second Injury" to Victims and Acute Response of Victims to Terror. *Evaluation and Change*, special issue, 1980.
7. Eitinger, Leo, and Axel Strom. *Mortality and Morbidity after Excessive Stress*. New York: Humanities Press, 1973.
8. Veterans Administration. *Study of Former Prisoners of War*. Washington, D.C.: U.S. Government Printing Office, May 1980.
9. Fields, Rona M. Victims of Terrorism: The Effects of Prolonged Stress. *Evaluation and Change*, special issue, 1980.
10. Keehan, Robert J. Follow-up Studies of World War II and Korean Conflict Prisoners. III Mortality to January 1, 1976. *American Journal of Epidemiology*, 3: February 1980.
11. Selye, Hans. *The Stress of Life*. New York: McGraw Hill, 1976.
12. Rahe, Richard H. Life-change Patterns Surrounding Illness Experience. *Journal of Psychosomatic Research*, 8: 1964.
13. Segal, Julius, Edna J. Hunter, and Zelda Segal. Universal Consequences of Captivity. *International Social Science Journal*, 28 (3): 1976.
14. Beebe, Gilbert W. Follow-up Studies of World War II and Korean War Prisoners. *American Journal of Epidemiology*, 101 (5): 1975.

Lifestyle Shock: The Psychological Experience of Being an American Prisoner of War in the Vietnam War

Charles A. Stenger

The following is an attempt to describe the profound psychological impact of being a POW. It is based on information and input from a number of sources: studies of POWs from World War II and Korea, U.S. Department of Defense interviews with Vietnam-era servicemen who escaped or were released, and the analyses of those knowledgeable in this area. It also reflects the views of the author who was a POW during World War II. Its purpose is to increase the understanding and sensitivity of anyone who may become involved in the lives of returned Vietnam POWs. While it should be considered a generally accurate portrayal of the realities and impact of life in a captive environment, it must be remembered that each POW is an individual whose experiences in captivity were unique to him alone.

PERSPECTIVE

The manner in which we humans live, work, play, and plan for tomorrow is of central importance to our existence. Through this lifestyle we seek to find meaning, direction, and fulfillment in life. Through it we function with reasonable confidence in our ability to cope with change, adversity, and threats to survival and with reasonable confidence that we can count on the support of our families, associates, and society.

What happens when that lifestyle is suddenly and completely altered? What happens when all of the things that sustained and gave direction to life are missing? What happens when this occurs because environmental forces, physical and social, no longer can be relied on to be supportive but instead are seen as unfamiliar, unpredictable, and hostile? This is the lifestyle shock of becoming a POW. It is also the lifestyle shock of later re-entering a world that psychologically had ceased to exist. It is made more complex by the fact that lifestyle shock also occurred for close family members of those who were captured—and it occurs again when the released POW comes home. It occurs in a very different way for families of those who were missing in action, for they lived for many years with the possibility that their relatives might come back and now must adjust to the reality that they will not.

INITIAL IMPACT OF BECOMING A POW

Almost from the moment of capture you have two devastating feelings. One, that it's the end of the world, that you have lost and will never again be a part of that world to which you really felt you belonged and counted for something. Second, an intense fear of death that never leaves you. You see your capturers as totally omnipotent and yourself as totally helpless. You know that any threat from him is a promise that could happen right now and you dare not challenge anything. Your confidence goes downhill radically almost immediately.

—A Vietnam POW

It is almost impossible to overstate the enormity of the meaning of captivity to the POW. This impact is heightened and deepened by his immediate isolation from other Americans and the desperately needed mutual reassurance this could bring. Self-esteem drops. The prisoner was somebody; now he is nothing. With it drops his confidence to cope with his environment. His fear of death is not panic but dread, based on the reality that he is valued not as a worthwhile human being but only a symbol of the "enemy." He feels that this "value" is tentative at best and may end at any moment, and his life along with it. He clings to the hope that he may survive this situation, but hope does not sustain him because he continually experiences the realities around him. He perceives himself as under the complete control of forces that are unconcerned about his survival, indifferent to his needs, aggressive, punitive, and totally unpredictable. As a result he sees himself as highly vulnerable, dependent, helpless, and lacking both in self-esteem and a sense of identity relevant to him in this alien world. He perceives other POWs as powerless, without status or influence, unsupportive, distant, and not really concerned about him. The shock of captivity dulls his sensitivity to stimuli and leaves him with an oppressive feeling of depression and resignation.

It is important to recognize that the complete loss of an active, responsible lifestyle that served to continually reaffirm self-worth, and its replacement by a passive compliant one that does not reinforce self-esteem, is the crux of the psychological change, not simply the fear of death, torture, or punishment.

THE PROCESS OF ADAPTATION TO THE CAPTIVE ENVIRONMENT

> When you are captured you have two choices, to survive or not survive. You have a total change in values; you relate everything to your chance of survival. You try to minimize harassment from guards by not challenging them; try to maintain the delicate balance of health and security. You don't dare think about home; it becomes too depressing afterwards. You become tremendous time-killers or have fantasies, talk to yourself, play games in which you become somebody who always succeeds and never fails. You gear down, slow everything down, and don't let yourself feel things very much.
>
> — A Vietnam POW

The solution to the problem of surviving psychologically as well as physically under conditions that permit only passive compliance is a complex one. Resignation to the physical environment of captivity, the adaptive response of following the rules all the time, and compliance with and acceptance of the numerous routines of prison life all maximize the likelihood of continued physical survival, as does an attitude of expecting to be disappointed in almost all things involving the captors, with a readiness to accept this. This avoids feelings of frustration and the danger of triggering other intense but inactive feelings.

"Gearing down" is the most popular way of describing the adaptive process. Attention that cannot be directed toward important activities is redirected. Simple acts such as folding a towel or blanket are repeated and prolonged to absorb attention in something "neutral." Doing these acts correctly also provides an important way of experiencing at least some degree of adequacy and success. This focusing on the immediate and the routine serves a protective function in that it enables the person to shut out more emotionally laden feelings, thoughts, and hopes. A near-total insulation from important feelings and wants prevails. The process causes the prisoner to become much less aware of and concerned about the passage of time. The focusing on the immediate environment and present moment enables the POW to avoid thinking about tomorrow and the world that means so much but is so totally inaccessible.

Time is filled, emotions are avoided, troubles are minimized, but what happens to self-esteem, to self-confidence? The repetitive acts of compliance to the routines of prison life and the lack of opportunity to perform meaningful activities gradually erode the POW's capacity to see himself in the active, self-responsible roles that made up his former life. Self-esteem is maintained to some degree by gratuitous, superficial, purposeful fantasies of seeing oneself in great roles in which adequacy, respect, status, and success in coping with every challenge are simultaneously experienced.

Social relations (basic human contacts with someone who shares one's interest, views, and so on) are similarly fabricated by those forced to live in isolation from other prisoners.

It is important to recognize that the POW has learned very well how to adapt to and endure a depriving, dehumanizing, and threatening environment. These adaptive mechanisms are consciously engaged in to preserve sanity. They are not symptoms of a breakdown of an effective reality orientation and behavioral response pattern. In fact, learning to endure the stress of imprisonment and to survive can have constructive as well as destructive psychological consequences. The POW is changed by his experiences. Personal growth in primary human values and the ability to tolerate frustration and disappointment is possible and does occur. But the damage has been done to an integrated, cohesive lifestyle for adapting in the environment and reintegrating with adaptive patterns in his own society.

THE PROCESS OF ADAPTATION TO FREEDOM

> Freedom is frightening and unreal. The freedom to choose simple alternatives can be a tremendous burden to carry. Adjustment is tough; you feel like a foreigner in your own world. You want to trust but are ready to retreat since you've learned to expect disappointment. However, if a "friendly" system lets him down, is oppressive, or keeps him in a state of uncertainty, it is more devastating to him and makes him cynical of *any* environment, or anyone else. You have to sort out your own life. You soon sense how far away you have been from a world you once took for granted.
>
> —A Vietnam POW

It is critical to recognize the devastating change in self-concept that has occurred and the conditions under which a positive self-image and lifestyle can be restored. The POW must be allowed a moment in time to reintegrate himself, to shed the extreme psychological defenses against inner feeling and outer stress that were necessary for survival in the captive environment, to re-establish his identity. Just as he felt immediately after capture, he again finds himself in a world in which he has no assured status, defined lifestyle, or active relationships with those around him. He recognizes that his relationship is historical and sentimental rather than relevant and current. And he is fearful that the image he presents will not be reacted to favorably. He must also have a moment to become aware of the events and changes that have occurred in his absence. There is a staggering gap between events in their homes, work, and society.

The capacity of the returned POW to deal with new stimuli is at first severely diminished. He had to "gear down" to survive; now he must "gear up" to assimilate and cope with the very high level of stimuli occurring in our modern society. A fairly extensive adjustment of values occurs within the individual during a long period of imprisonment. He will have new views of old situations, and we must expect a collision between the different sets of values.

IMPLICATIONS

To be helpful to the returned POW and his family, an empathic understanding of how the prisoner has been living is crucial. Returned POWs are very much concerned that no one will understand what it was like. Communication is also crucial in the need for accurate feedback. After years of living with uncertainty, they need straightforward answers, good or bad. Where sincerity or credibility are in doubt, the opportunity to be of help to the POW is greatly reduced. Interpersonal interactions must be not only emphatic and honest; they must also be open and informative rather than authoritarian and directive. The returned POW needs time, room, and options so that he can play an increasingly active role in the process of re-establishing himself as a valued and worthwhile person to his family, his environment, and himself.

PART ONE

THE FIRST CAPTURED

Gen. George Patton was once quoted as saying that "fixed fortifications are monuments to the stupidity of man." Nowhere was that truer for U.S. forces than in the Asiatic Theater of Operations during World War II, where 17,000 American troops were captured by the Japanese in the first five months of the war. These men were also the first American POWs taken. Their incarcerations lasted the longest, in some cases more than 44 months, which sets these men apart from any other World War II U.S. POWs. The length of imprisonment and the effects of Japanese torture often had severe repercussions for the captives.

John Emerick

John Emerick enlisted in Pittsburgh, Pennsylvania, and was part of the peacetime army stationed in the Philippines when the Japanese attacked on December 8, 1941. After several months of fighting in the jungles of Bataan, John surrendered along with other U.S. servicemen, most of whom suffered from severe malnutrition, on April 8, 1942. He survived a Death March and other torture by his Japanese captors, witnessing hundreds of atrocities that stay with him until this day. Because of these nightmares, which still haunt him, he hasn't had a good night's sleep since his incarceration nearly 50 years ago. As well, he begins to shake uncontrollably when he speaks of the past. His story begins with his capture by a Japanese tank, the commander of which was educated in the United States and spoke fluent English.

So we told him, "Hey, you guys have been chasing us around these jungles for four or five days. How about something to eat?"

So he threw down this big can of peaches that they took from the Americans. Best goddamned can of peaches that I ever ate in my life. And then he wrote us up a pass.

And he said, "Razor your gun, your ammunition, anything that could be used as a weapon, or you won't be safe. You will have to go to the Mariveles to surrender. Do you know where it is?"

We just nodded and then started out. When we got there, there was already a lot of troops already there. The first thing I saw was this poor guy laying down there. It looked like someone had used a sabre to cut his head off. I later found out that he had had a yen hidden on his person, positive proof that he had either killed or robbed a Jap or both. This is how the Japanese dealt with such acts.

Then I said to myself, "Oh Christ, we are really in trouble. These people aren't human."

Shortly after, we started the [Bataan] Death March, eight abreast. It looked like when they first started that we were only going to be driven a little way up the road. But by the time we got to about the third day, we knew they were just hoping all of us would die. Hell, they hadn't even given us a drink of water. By then the people really started to fall out. A guy would jump into a ditch for a little bit of water. They they'd run a bayonet through you, or shoot you or hit you in the head with a shovel, whatever way they could to dispose of you. Behind us they had a cordon of tanks. If you stopped, those tanks would ground you into the dirt. The Japs also had this group we called the Buzzard Squad. They killed those that couldn't keep up.

In one case this poor old bastard GI simply kneeled down and opened up his shirt and begged for them to shoot him. He couldn't take it anymore. They fired a couple of rounds into the guy, but he wasn't dead. Then they made us stand there and watch them as they dug a hole to bury the guy alive. I won't tell you the guy's name, but one of our guys hit the poor bastard on the head to put him out of his misery. I thought one of the Japs was going to kill him for doing that, but they let him go. They had already had their fun.

After the march, they put us in boxcars. Boxcars in the Philippines are a quarter of inch plate; and they jammed you in there so tight that if somebody died you didn't know he was dead till he fell flat on his face after they let you out. I remember getting into that boxcar. . . . Next thing I remember was arriving at Camp O'Donnell. I was standing with a bamboo pole across my shoulders to get water from the one lone spigot in camp, and this goddamned Jap came and pushed me and then kicked my canteens away from me. Then he pushed me out toward the gate with ten other people, and forced me into a truck with five other people. I said out loud, "What's the son of a bitch going to do?" That is the way I referred to the Japanese.

Then he spoke to me in Japanese, and I said, "I wish I knew what this son of a bitch was saying to me."

He said, "I mean sit down, and you call me that again and I'll shoot you."

From that day on I learned to speak pretty good Japanese. But that little son of a bitch saved my life, because he chose me to go to another location where I would be made to clean and repair barges.

The guys we worked for were Japanese marines, and any food they had left after every meal they would ship it over to us, which was more than we could have even expected at O'Donnell. What you have to understand is already our rations were cut so severe that we were emaciated. Also, all of us were going downhill with malaria and everything else, dysentery, all that. Dysentery in camp was especially bad. Guys were dying faster than you could bury them. After these Jap marines cut out, I was shipped to different prison camps all over the islands, but each time it was the same old shit.

The worst camp I was in I believe was Hanawa in Japan. You had to walk four miles up a mountain, through waist deep snow on this real narrow path. If you slipped off and slid down into one of the snow banks they would never be able to find you. The snow was that deep. I spent fourteen months up there. They had a good union there, though. You got a ration of rice. If you worked and you brought out four cars of copper, you got another ration. Another four cars, you got another ration. That was how each day went. If you didn't work, they didn't feed you and your stomach collapsed and you died. They then would carry you down and put you on a pile with all the other corpses and cover you with a tarp. They couldn't bury them cause the ground was frozen.

The snow was so deep we were given those big straw shoes so we wouldn't slip down through the snow. The only time your feet weren't completely frozen was when you put them on, but you had to take them off when you went in the mine. Those sons of bitches. They aren't human. Nobody can tell me they're human.

A female Army correspondent was asking me what we should do with Japan now that the war was over. You know, we were just bullshitting, and I don't remember where it was, Manila or wherever, yeah, it was Manila after I'd been released. I said, "What we ought to do is take all the GIs out of there and then level the whole fucking place. Don't leave anything there. Burn the little bastards out." The younger people of this country are the ones that are going to suffer for us not doing that. No doubt about it.

But to get from the Philippines to Japan, they shipped us over by boat. We were shipped out before the war ended. By that time the tide of the war had really changed and we controlled both the sea and land, which was good as a whole, but bad for our journey. When we left Manila, U.S. ships chased us to Java. There were 54 ships in the convoy I was in. It took us 32 days to go from the Philippine Islands to Japan.

People were losing their minds during this time because we were all locked below in a hold—no accessible food, water, or light. We waited to the very last minute to send anyone topside that died, usually until they started to smell so bad that you could no longer stand it, and they were falling like flies. That way we could get their ration of rice and water for the day. Your mind just couldn't comprehend how bad things were. I still can't believe it and I was there. Cannibalism, the works.

When we got to Japan, they shipped us up to the very northern point. From the tropics into that cold weather. It took a lot of people. Finally, we just started gathering bits of wood in the nearby forests to bury the bodies. Then the Japs gave us these little boxes to put some of the ashes in and the guys' dog tags. When we were liberated, we just handed the boxes over to our guys.

I will never forget that liberation date. We got bombed. About 37 were killed. I don't know how many were hurt, but there was a hell of a lot of people busted up. Some of them died. Some of them, if they lasted long enough to get medical attention, lived. We were hit by our own dive bombers. The Japs wouldn't allow us to dig any foxholes. Instead, they made us sit in the middle of the compound like pigeons.

But in Hannawa, all the buildings are made of wood. Our guys hit them with incendiary-type bombs. It was a firestorm which sucked all the oxygen out of the place. That killed a hell of a lot of people. If they didn't burn to death, they suffocated.

Right afterwards, first thing you know, somebody is hollering that the war is over. Then our own guys flew by, dropping leaflets on us telling us that the war was over. Then our planes started dropping these large, bomb-looking food tubes down to us. When they hit, they almost sounded like a dead bomb. Then we couldn't get them open. Goddamned things.

But out of all the bullshit I went through, the trip over to Japan was the worst. There were so many people that you couldn't lay down. You had to sit all the time. And the food, you were like an animal. You would fight your best friend for his water or his food. It was survival of the fittest. It defies description. When we got by Java they took us out. There were ulcers all over my body. They took a water hose, hosed you down just to clean you up a bit. There was crap all over you. You had dysentery, everybody had dysentery. Even when our guys flew us from Japan to Okinawa, the pilot said, "You guys must be shitting all over this airplane." Everybody laughed.

The attacks on us by U.S. ships and planes was just horrible. There we were, locked in those hell holes below the water line, and you could hear the attacking aircraft topside, the torpedoes whipping through the water and other ships being hit and sunk. We were completely helpless. Guys were screaming and crying, praying, anything they could do to get through it. There weren't any atheists with us on that trip.

I'm stilled pissed off about everything that happened. We lost a lot of good boys, and never had to. MacArthur wouldn't let Skinny Wainwright cut loose with the 26 or so different outfits he had to counterattack the Japs when they first landed. MacArthur never told the Navy what the hell he was doing. He just pulled out of Manila as fast as he could. The Navy was really pissed off at him.

After that, after our capture, we were nothing but slaves to the Japs. If they needed you somewhere they just herded you into trucks or boxcars like cattle and shipped you there. To them, you were expendable. They wanted to annihilate you. They treated me like that all the time. I was there until we finally dropped the bomb. Then things started to change a bit. They got scared of us. They knew they were goners if they didn't treat us right.

I only remember one good thing from my whole time there. I was working, and I was using something like a hydraulic jack. Well, I was setting up and I was by myself. The Jap that was guarding me was getting some other slaves to load the copper on a ship. Out of nowhere, a Jap woman came up to me and stuck an apple in my hand, then ran away. That was the best damn apple I ever ate in my life. I often thought if I could have found out who that woman was, I would send her the damn nicest fruit basket you ever saw.

I weighed about 180 lbs. when I was captured, and 98 lbs. when I was liberated. I lost a lot of my weight, though, before I was captured on Bataan when we were starving to death. I used to weigh 200 lbs, but I dropped a quick 20 there. Our rations had been cut to literally nothing. I remember my Christmas dinner of that year being only a half of a can of sardines. And then we got our rations cut beyond that a few times as well. Right after that, with our weakened conditions, the diseases started—malaria first, then black water fever, dingy fever, dysentery. Pellagra started to take its toll; tropical ulcers all over your body. You just had no resistance. Then the Death Marches came. The people that survived the Death Marches—somebody else was looking out for them. It wasn't them. Me, I don't believe I did it.

I survived, I think, because I built up such a hatred, which I have been told by a psychiatrist. But if I ever see the son of a bitch who took my canteen away on the Death March, then took my helmet and poured a drink and gave it to his horse, I'll get him. I was lucky that I was able to get another canteen from another guy.

Today on the way in here, they were playing a song on the radio about Pearl Harbor. We had a song over there, too: "The Battling Brats of Bataan." "No mamma, no papa, no Uncle Sam." What the hell is the rest? I don't remember. "Nothing in the pot. I am just a hungry bastard that the nation has forgot." That is what we used to sing. So these are the songs we had over there. Then what used to irk the hell out of a lot of us was what Tokyo Rose used to say when she did her bit. The Japs had loudspeakers all along the front lines, and they'd play this shit to us all the time on Bataan. They'd play songs like "Who Is Kissing Her Now." And they'd say things like, "How do you know who your wife is sleeping with tonight?" And stuff about how she's getting tired of waiting for the ship that will never come in. All that stuff irked the troops, and a lot of them used to take that to heart. Me, I just thought it was good music because they had better records than we had.

After the war, I was taken out of Japan, sometime in September and we came through Nagasaki. Then we got on an aircraft carrier and they took us from there to Okinawa. We stayed there a day, and then they took us on B-24s and B-29s to the Philippines. On the way there we kept losing engines until finally we made an emergency landing. From there they put us on a cargo plane and flew us right into Clark Field, where we stayed about three weeks. I developed an ear problem, so they had to keep me an extra two weeks or so. By the time I got back to the States it was sometime in November.

In San Francisco, they herded us like a bunch of undesirables off the ship. They had guards on both sides of the gangplank and buses that had the drapes drawn. And they took us right to the hospital. They wouldn't let us talk to anybody. We weren't allowed to communicate to a damn soul, like we were a bunch of undesirables. They took us there, and they kept us there for a few days. And then they shipped us across the country to Wilson, Va., in a hospital train. There again, the shades were drawn. We weren't allowed to associate with anybody all along the way. When we got to the Wilson Hospital, we had no examinations, none at all. It was just a preliminary thing. They tested and found out I had bad eyes. I had lost my eyesight in a concentration camp because of poor nutrition, and I told them that. So they examined my eyes. They gave me a pair of glasses, but that was the only kind of physical I was given. We stayed there for a while and then they shipped me home, around sometime in November. I know I was home for Christmas. Then I had to go back. But this was how they treated us—like a bunch of undesirables.

I got married in February of '46. But when I first came home, I really hit the bottle. I was drunk all the time. It was the only way I could calm my nerves. Or was it guilt? Why did I survive and someone else didn't? I really couldn't tell you. Was it a combination? I just tried to forget. That is what you try to do. But I can't tell you what prompted it. For all the time we were in the 29th replacement depot at Clark Field, they gave us soft foods, and when we all got home, we were bloated. They just wanted to make us look better for the folks back home. I weighed 210 pounds when I got home. I weighed 86 pounds when I got out of the camp, and I put all that weight on in less than a year. They had to give us special uniforms we had gotten so big.

The whole situation about how we were captured, how we were treated, how MacArthur handled the whole thing, was a big joke. One month before we were bombed, we were told that the Japanese were expected to try and land airborne troops on Nicholas and Clark Field and at different bases. The military knew for months, but they didn't do anything about it. Then when the Japs did attack, our B-19s were lined up all nice and neat for them just to take out.

I don't know why we acted so stupidly. I think the brass wanted to get the American people to do something because Germany was moving pretty fast and we had to do something quick. They just wanted to jack up the American people so they would fight the Germans and that is exactly what they did. But when we came home, I think they were ashamed of something, because it was 40 years later before they chose to recognize that we even existed. We couldn't file a claim for assistance from the Veterans Administration until the early 1980s.

But the whole goddamned thing was a mess, like our government had planned for it to go down the way that it did. Hell, MacArthur knew that we had broken the Jap's code. I believe he knew what they were going to do every step along the way. I just felt that Roosevelt gave him orders to let them take the Philippines, to let American boys be fired on, so the country would want to join the fight.

Again, it was like we sabotaged our own entire effort. We left all our food and supplies just piled up on the docks for the Japs to take. Our enemy lived off our supplies for nearly the entire campaign while we starved. Then we were just handed over to the Japs.

Here's the situation. You surrendered to the Japs, period. If you don't obey the orders to surrender, you will be court-martialed, period. No one wanted to be court-martialed, so you surrendered. We didn't know at the time, though, how cruel the Japs were going to be. And you didn't want to try and escape after you surrendered because the Japs put you in these ten-men death squads. If one guy escaped, they shot the other nine. MacArthur knew what was going to happen to us, though. You going to tell me he didn't know? The order to surrender, to retreat, everything, it all came from the high command. The high command is the one who should shoulder the blame for all that happened. They should have looked after us before, during, and after the war. If a few of their doctors would have fully documented our conditions and what happened to us, no way we would have been fit to work. But we had to, and we suffered as a result, because they wouldn't even acknowledge that we had problems, or in some cases, even that we existed.

There isn't anyone of us that there isn't something wrong with, but we had to wait nearly 40 years to get someone to acknowledge that there may have been even something wrong with us. Two psychiatrists gave me a physical, and they couldn't believe what they found. They told me that I couldn't work, that I was a walking, emotional time bomb. One minute I can be nice and calm, and then something triggers me, then I blow up. And another thing is my night terrors. Forty-some years later, every dream I have, there is a Jap in it. I wake up two or three times a month in a cold sweat. The best I could hope for was getting 15 to 20 minutes of sleep before I'd wake up. For 40 years, that's how I slept. I was always scared to death of some Jap sneaking up on me and slitting my throat. I've been taking a real strong sleeping pill since I got back from seeing that psychiatrist in Texas. It just knocks me out. It works two out of every three nights.

All the damage done to my nervous system as the result of my beriberi didn't help either. It screws up your whole system. We used to stand in knee deep snow in Japan just to try to numb the pain. It got so bad that somebody could just point at you and you'd scream.

One of the reasons the Japs beat on us was because we were real tall people. They just beat the hell out of us. This is the worst time of the year for me, around Christmas and Memorial Day, you know. It is a bad time. I start thinking about people I was with and the first thing I know I am crying. I'll tell you one thing. No one will take me to a prison camp again. They might carry me, but I won't walk.

But if one of my comrades from the Death March died, I'd cry like a baby. Yet we were such animals though. If you woke up and the guy next to you was dead, looking up at the sky, all you cared about was his shoes and pants. We weren't human anymore. None of us could cry anymore. With all the death and despair around us, still nothing would come out. That's still true today, unless one of the guys die. Then we cry like babies. But we were like zombies over there, we just did.

Every time I have one of my panic or terror attacks, it always relates back to something that happened over there. Some incident back there triggers my subconscious and the first thing you know, I'm in tears, and I don't know why the hell I'm crying. But when I'm in the company of some of the guys that were over there, it's different.

We drove from Pittsburgh to Port Clinton, Ohio, about a month ago, the four of us went—Ken, his wife, and me and my wife. One of our guys up there died, and a lot of us got together to pay our respects and bullshit. A situation like that is different, but if you were just to meet me and talk to me for five minutes, I'd be climbing the walls almost immediately looking for a way out.

There is only so much the human mind can take. If a movie or show comes on TV that triggers something in my subconscious that is somehow related to what happened back then, it throws me all out of whack. I get the shakes. I can't sleep. I'm not good for at least two weeks. When I got home, things weren't much better for us. I mean, no one could understand us. I'll tell you it was a shock. My mother couldn't make enough for me. She would have bacon and eggs, everything, and I just couldn't get enough. I was engaged in 1939, and I got married in 1945. I went right to work. Right after work, I would go right to the bar. Then I would come home around six o'clock, eat nothing, then booze it.

I went into heavy construction when I first got back. I went to Duquesne University, and then to United States Steel where I had five different jobs, four different plant operations. It took me five years to complete my required courses at Duquesne. How the hell I did all that work with all my drinking I'll never know. I don't know whether it was the booze that helped me or not, but I came out of there with pretty high marks. I went right to the Bureau of Mines and I was general foreman in the area of metal research. I had a big job. I stayed there 32 years, but there was four years in there, early on, when I drank so much that I didn't know what the hell day it was. How I got through all that four years, I don't know.

Then one day my dad called me up and said, "You are going to church with me today."

"Why do you want me to go to church for?" I asked. One thing I didn't want was for him to talk to me. He sat me down and straightened me up that day. That is it. That is where I slowed down. Then I didn't drink for about three years. Then this other guy from World War II and I started to sneak drinks into the mill with us. That was about all that I learned from my experience with the Japs was how to scheme, because you had to always stay one step ahead of the Japs to keep from getting killed. Other than that, other than the loss of my health and nerves, that's all I got. And the country didn't even start giving us our due until in '81 or '82.

My biggest regret is the men who died and maybe wouldn't have if they would have acknowledged our situation earlier. I still work for that cause today. That's my main purpose—to try to get things done for those who are still alive, and for the widows and families of those who are dead. If it helps somebody, it might be worth it.

The only thing people talk about today is Pearl Harbor. Nobody talks about how we got wiped out at Nichols Field. The bodies, the arms, and legs we threw up in the dump truck and took them to a hole, dumped them out, saved the dog tags, and covered them up with a dozer—they won't talk about that. In London, they have more history books written on what really happened to us than we have here. Nobody really believes that what we say happened to us could have ever taken place.

We're still fighting now for our rights to tell the true story of what really happened. We just don't know any better. We are fighting a losing battle, but we won't quit. If we could complete this, maybe some people will open their eyes. If the government would have given us something, and not just forgot about us, we both, and they, would have been further ahead. They wouldn't have needed all the doctors, they wouldn't have needed all the nurses they need now. They would have been way ahead. But we've always been a hidden element of society and we continue to be so. And, like I say, it hurts everybody. There are a lot of pictures showing the Holocaust and other elements of the war, but you'd be pretty hard-pressed to find anything on how they butchered us in the Death March or what they did to us in one of their camps. And this country deserted us and then we get back and they forget about us. That is the hard part. The same thing happened in the Vietnam War, with exception of being spat upon. They treated us like lepers. They shunned us at every chance they got. They didn't believe what we had to say. They just wouldn't listen. We tried to bring this to the public so they wouldn't forget, because it very well could happen again, again, and again.

I told you this before. If you look in the library in the history section under December 7, 1941, you'll find a lot of material. But on May 6 in the Philippines, there is very little. One of the things that was hard for us to make people believe was another human would treat another human like the Japanese treated us. You couldn't make them believe it. And there's no way that anyone is going to listen more now than they did before, because the Japanese are too influential.

Ken Curley

Ken Curley, like John Emerick, originally enlisted in Pittsburgh, Pennsylvania, and was part of the peacetime army in the Philippines as well. He was captured on Corregidor. He was able to survive over 42 months of imprisonment by the Japanese because, he claims, of his profound hatred for his captors. Like Emerick, he suffers from severe postwar trauma. His story begins with his entrance into the service.

Work was scarce; there was hardly any to be had. So I enlisted in the early part of '41, and I went overseas later that year. First, we landed in Hawaii for refueling and supplies. They were going to take me off the ship there and put me in the MPs there because I was tall. They were always trying to get MPs over six feet. Somehow, I got out of that. Then we cast off, and I had a little fight on board ship. What happened was a company of eight or nine engineers got on the ship, and they were looking for a place to bunk. I guess they were going to try and outrank us and take our bunks. This one engineer then came up and sat on my bunk, and said to me, "I guess I'll take this bunk. It looks like a good one."

I said, "Over a pig's ass you will. Get your ass off there or I am going to throw you overboard."

I used to be able to handle myself pretty well. When my guys saw me doing that they followed suit. We had a bunch of guys from New York. We had a Lieutenant Walters; he was from Pittsburgh. And some one went over and told him, "You better come over 'cause Curley is going to throw one of these new engineers out through the window."

He finally came over and quieted everybody down.

When we got to the Philippines, because I was such a hardass they wanted to take me off the ship and make me a guard of a leper colony. I told them that I was already assigned. When I got away from that, there were some non-coms on the dock, and they were asking if there was anyone around that played baseball. I said that I did, and so I was assigned to Battery Company A, which is also where I stayed, even though I took my boot training in Battery C. When I got into Battery A, I was on the football team, the boxing team, and of course the baseball team. We had to take a lot of courses in artillery. Eventually, I became a cannoneer. But a short time after the war came along, they made me a machine gunner. When the Jap bombers finally came over, they were so high we couldn't hit them with our machine guns. The artillery people used the 42-second fuses on their munitions to get at them. But after the fuses ran out, we weren't able to hit them with anything. They would come by and drop their bombs. We were totally defenseless. It was terrible.

On this one time they made a pass at us and then swung around to hit us a second time. Someone in another tower, the one closest to me, screamed, "Bill Bragg got hit."

So I got on the phone real quick with the battery commander. He asked for my opinion of the situation. I told him about Bragg getting hit but I couldn't tell him with what. I didn't know if it was shrapnel from a bomb or from some shattered stones. All I knew was that there was a whole bunch of stuff flying around.

On their second pass, this Italian fellow who I was on the tower with was standing up with binoculars, looking out at a plane coming straight for us. I screamed at him, "Get your dead ass down," and just then a bomb hit and we wound up on the ground. God, it was terrible. They were still dropping bombs all around us. We crawled down to our tunnel as fast as possible. Then, just as I crossed the gun emplacement, a bomb hit our gun. I scrambled inside the door of a degassing chamber. As soon as I got inside another bomb hit, which threw me up against a door. I was chewing tobacco at the time, and I must have swallowed it because I don't know what happened to it. Anyway, when I got inside, someone grabbed me and said, "You're wounded." I was blood from head to foot, yet I just kept running down through our tunnel. I was just too scared to stop and look at my wounds.

From there they took me to the hospital, which was in the tunnel. After I recuperated I was able to walk around for a while, and go outside and get a little air. But I couldn't stand just being cooped up, so they put me back on duty. In March they shipped me over to Bataan, up on Mariveles I got wounded up there again, so from there, that was around seven to ten days, they sent me down to a field hospital. When I got there it had just been bombed and there were patients hanging in the trees with their arms blown off, bodies all over the place. The Japanese didn't believe in honoring the Red Cross or neutrality of the hospitals. From there, because they couldn't take care of me, I was shipped back to Corregidor. A couple of days after I left Bataan, it fell. That was on April 9, 1942. From then on, the bombings and shellings increased on Corregidor until May 6, when we surrendered and they took us down to an airstrip, where they herded all the prisoners who had surrendered. Before we were herded down there, there was an Army messenger that came by to all our positions to tell us that at 12 o'clock, Corregidor would surrender, and to get rid of all your arms, destroy any weapons that you can. So we were going to blow up the 12-foot gun that I was manning by putting a dummy round in it and setting it off, but one of the officers stopped us because he said the Japs would get mad. As a prisoner, one of the first details the Japs put me on was their grave detail. We had to go and pick up all the dead Japanese, then they'd cut off one arm of each of the dead, and that part they'd burn separately, then put the ashes in a little urn with the dog tags and identification and send home. The rest of the body they set on like a bonfire, and we burned them that way. We were there for a couple of weeks. Not too much longer afterwards, they were marching us God knows where until we walked through where the Japanese were loading all the food that they confiscated from Corregidor. Then they took us to some point nearby where we marched all the way down the highway, Dewey Boulevard I think it was called. There is a new name to it now, though. We marched the entire length of the boulevard down to a prison. Right along side of me the whole time was a full colonel, a Colonel Bunker. He was a regional commander. I looked over at him and he was getting real red. The heat was really getting to him. I asked him, "Would you like me to carry your bag, sir?"

He just snarled at me and said, "I'll carry my own, thank you, soldier." He must have had it full of booze or money or something.

So we walked to Bilibid. But on the way, you couldn't be marched 25 feet without some Jap searching you. If you had Japanese money on you, and you didn't give it to them, you were dead. If you had rings on and you couldn't get them off, they cut off your fingers. So you damn well better take them off. If you had gold teeth, they would knock them out. You couldn't march any more than 25 or 50 feet without someone searching you. So we didn't have any wallets. We didn't have any identification of any kind. We didn't have any canteens. We didn't have anything by the time we got to the prison. We stayed overnight there. Then the next morning, they marched us out to the train depot and put us in boxcars. They must have put 100 men in a boxcar. I think that 25 would have been a little more comfortable. But 100 in each one, we were like sardines. If someone passed out, they couldn't fall to the floor. If they died, they died standing up.

From there they took us to the San Fernando Valley, then to the Cappas. And they unloaded us there. Then they marched us from there to Camp Three Cabanatuan.

God knows it was hot. They changed guards pretty often, so they were always fresh and mean and moved us along at a quick pace. We got searched. We got the hell knocked out of us. This all happened with no food, no water, and we marched all the way to Cabanatuan. When we got up to Cabanatuan, we were there for a short while. I was assigned to a wood-cutting detail, which gave me a chance to get away from camp so I could scrounge around and finagle with the natives. The Japanese thought I was talking to, conferring with guerrillas, so they took me back to camp and they hog-tied me, forcing me into a squatting position with a two-inch pole behind my knees. Every time the Nips thought I wasn't putting all my weight on the pole, they would sit on my shoulders and bounce up and down. I was left like that for days, and every time I fell over they would set me backup and knock the shit out of me, I really don't know how long I was like that because I lost consciousness of it. All I could think of was, 'If I could get you, you son of a bitch, I would strangle you.' After they finally untied me, I couldn't walk. They had to pick me up and walk me around a little at a time until my circulation came back.

They were cruel bastards. Once three guys escaped and they caught them shortly after just walking up the road. They probably didn't have the strength to do much else. When they brought them back in camp they made these guys dig their own graves while the whole camp just stood by and watched. Then the Japs just shot them, one by one, which forced each to their knees. Then the Jap who was in charge of the firing squad went over and shot each in the head again so they'd fall straight into their graves. That was just the way that it was dealing with the Japs; they believed in mass punishment. They believed that if you saw an atrocity, that it would give you second thoughts. Finally they broke up the camp because there wasn't all that many people there, after sending men to Japan after being sold into slavery. And they took us down to another camp, where they had a farm detail. The things that were grown there were supposed to be used for the benefit of the prisoners. But instead the Japanese troops were fed from our efforts and we got nothing but lugao.

On one of the wood-chopping details we spotted a herd of Brahman bulls. So the Japs tried to shoot one of them but couldn't. So one of our guys said I will show you how to do it, and knocked one right off. The Japs must have tasted the meat and liked it because they captured this whole herd and moved it down to our camp. But somehow the Hindus, the Indians, got wind of it and they wouldn't allow them to slaughter them because the Brahman was their sacred cow.

Then I was shipped off to Nichols Field to be part of the airstrip-rebuilding duty. It was a real brutal detail, so brutal of a detail that some guys tried to break their own arms just to get out of it. You weren't allowed to wear shoes, so the Japs made fun out of kicking you in the ankles. The detail was run by a guy we called the White Angel. Some people said he was German and other said he was a Nip marine. But I think he was in the Japanese Navy, and he was a mean son of a bitch, and all his guards were too. So anyway, I stayed on that detail until I got malaria so bad that they had to ship me back to camp. After I recovered from malaria, they shipped me out on a bridge-building detail.

One night, the camp was raided by Philippine guerrillas. A couple of men, I think there were three, took off with these guerrillas. The next morning they had *toco*, which is roll call, and they made you count off. It just so happened that these two brothers used to stand side-by-side during roll call. When the three guys escaped, the Japs started shooting the remaining members on their ten-man shooting squads. The one brother was left to live, but he had to watch his brother die in front of him. Supposedly, they were both orphans and used to always talk about what they were going to do after they got home. The Japs didn't care. To them you were no better than the Brahman cows they shot for meat, maybe even less worthy.

In '44 I was finally shipped off to Japan. They just herded us into the holds of these ships as fast as they could. The way you landed when you hit was the way you stayed the rest of the trip. The holds were loaded with horse manure; they had just unloaded the calvary and never cleaned out the holds.

A lot of guys went over the edge during our trip, with 700 of us crammed into one of those little holds and all. Guys were dying like flies. Some guys even wanted to die. They'd just lay down in their own slop and declare that they were going to have to be carried out of there. But we wouldn't put up with that bullshit, so we would do anything to make them mad, to get them to fight us, to get that old fighting spirit going in them again. God knows how long I was on that ship, but it seemed like forever. With the American Navy controlling the sea, they had to maneuver around quite a bit. They kept leaving, then coming back to the same port until they finally decided to take a zig-zag course to Japan.

I was in Japan about a year, maybe a little more. They took us north to our camp in trains after we docked. We were sent to Camp Three, which was the worst camp, I heard. They had some mean sons of bitches there. The work area I worked in supposedly was one of the sites for one of the A-bombs if another would have been dropped. We had to march three miles, in our weakened conditions, to work every day because the Americans were bombing so often that they had to hide the train that they rode us in in a tunnel, and the tunnel was three miles away from where we worked. Then when the Americans did bomb, we had to try and run three miles back to that tunnel to protect ourselves. The bombing would scare the shit out of the guards, but they had to stay with you. So if you didn't run during the bombing raids they'd beat you.

I was on a duty for stacking stones for loading into a kiln at the time. But I was so weak I was having a hard time lifting the stones. I got beat during this time, too, with an iron pole.

The first winter I was there, it got down to about 20 degrees below zero, and I didn't have any shoes. Finally they gave me a pair of tennis shoes. Then I stole a pair of mittens, cut out the thumbs and sewed up the cuff and used those inside my tennis shoes. But I got caught doing it and I got beat so bad. But yet I went back and stole another pair. It was the only way I could survive. Then I went in scrounging around one day and I found they had a kiln that had a bunch of colanders in it, and it was filled with seawater. They were dehydrating, evaporating the water off it to get the salt, so I stole some salt.

We worked seven days a week, about 15 or 16 hours a day. We never had a day off the whole time we were there except one day. The International Red Cross was coming through to investigate the camps, to inspect them, so they gave us a day off so we could clean everything up. And they gave us one piece of steam bread. It was the only time that I had bread there. They used to give us one little bucket of coal a day to heat our barracks, and that was for a place that was about 100 feet long. So we used to steal and then sneak coal back into the barracks. But they checked us down every night on the way in, and if you got caught with any coal, they'd really beat the shit out of you.

That little stove, outside of the kiln we worked in front of, was the only heat we had. But going from the extreme heat of the kilns to the extreme cold on the outside and our detail killed a lot of guys. I got pneumonia two or three times while I was over there. This happened in Camp No. 1 Cabanatuan while I was there. Guys were dying at about 100 to 150 a day. We couldn't even dig the graves fast enough. There were guys that were out on the grave detail in the morning and were buried in the same graves that afternoon. That is how fast they were dying.

Before the war, I met this one priest from the Pittsburgh area, Father Bauman, who was over there. This happened before we were captured on Corregidor. During those constant Jap bombings, this priest would get there alongside this makeshift altar, and he would just stand there when the rest of us would be scrambling for cover. Hell, if I could've found a sheet of cigarette paper I would have got under it. But I'll never forget that priest. Father Bauman was from a Pittsburgh suburb, same as I was.

But anyway, back in Japan, I eventually just kept working in that brick factory. They gave us three bowls of rice a day, but the bowls were only the size of a baseball. That's all we got.

I remember when the first A-bomb was dropped. We really didn't know what happened. But I do remember how the Japs just kept talking about how the Americans didn't play fair, so it must have been devastating. That's all we thought. Again, either the second bomb was supposed to be dropped on Arao where we worked, or a later one if the Japs didn't surrender. But the Americans never got to that. They just saturated us with conventional stuff. A few days after the second bomb was dropped, the war was over, and our planes flew over dropping notes to us, telling us that they would be sending a recovery team for us soon.

In the factory where I worked there was this Japanese girl working there. One day a couple of the boys came up to me with her picture and said that she wanted to see me. So I used to stop by to see her regularly on the way to the *benjo*, meaning restroom, and she'd give me bits of rice and a cigarette every now and then. So when the Americans started to drop those food packages to us, on those nylon parachutes, I was going to return the favor to her. But when I went back to find her, her office was completely flattened. I don't know whether she ever lived or not.

We left Japan sometime in September. I always thought it was too soon to go through Nagasaki. It had only been bombed in August. But they took us through the damn town. I hated the Red Cross to begin with. On one corner the Salvation Army was offering coffee and doughnuts free, on the other side the Red Cross was selling them. They took us there and they deloused us. They just took all our clothes off, and we could take a bath and then they issued new clothes. So one day we are staying there and I said to one of the guys, I said, "What the hell is that over there?" So I got my canteen and went over to a line that was forming, and they poured out rum for all their sailors, but refused to give any to me.

Then they took us to Okinawa. We were out at sea when the typhoon hit, so we anchored in a bay. Then we took off again, and a second typhoon hit. Finally, they shipped us back off to the Philippines by plane, and they fed us like heck, trying to fatten us up before being shipped home. But it was a mess getting back to the States. Our ship, named U.S. Marine Shark, broke down. We had trouble in Hawaii. So when we finally landed in San Francisco, we were shipped by hospital train to Letterman General Hospital in Stanton, Virginia, but I kept bugging them. All I really wanted to do was to go home. I hadn't been there in six or seven years.

So I came home after I finally got a furlough from the Woodrow Wilson Hospital in Stanton, Virginia. There were three or four of us who made the drive to Indian Town Gap, Pennsylvania. That was sometime in November. Then after a few weeks I got a notice that I was to report to a camp in Indiana to pick up my discharge papers. So I took a train there, but they didn't have any records when I arrived. So I had to hang around and wait for them—two weeks—and I only brought with me the clothes on my back. So they gave me a clean, new uniform every day and I'd send home the one I'd worn the previous day. Other than that, they didn't know who the hell I was—the story of my life. I had no identification, no nothing. When I went into the service they lost my records. Then they lost my records again, and then again. I couldn't understand why something as important as a military record wasn't kept in a safe place. There should be records in half a dozen places so if they caught on fire or got bombed they would still have records someplace. So I wrote them a letter and I asked them about keeping records on microfilm. They said they never thought of it. I was very disgusted with the entire process by the time I got out, and it was also tough for us to tell anyone what we had really been through, because there was just no way they could understand.

One of the things that was hard for us to make people believe was that one human would treat another human the way the Japanese treated us. We could not make them believe it. With the Holocaust they have a lot of pictures, they can show that in a movie. They did not show anything about how they butchered you on a Death March, or the way they killed you in the camps. The Japanese are too influential right now. They don't want to upset them. A professor from Duquesne University said he was trying to get my story published in the *Pittsburgh Press*. They told him that my story was too controversial and it would upset the Japanese, thus they would not publish it. Now that is a kick in the ass, I'll tell you.

The war with those little yellow bastards still goes on, but in a much different form. We helped them build up their steel industry and let our steel industry go to hell. We don't have any steel mills to speak of in this country, and as a result of that, we have no coal mines to speak of. The stuff that they sell us is inferior. That brings up another story. I think it is the most asinine thing that they could possibly do, that they could make a spaceship and put foreign parts in, and every damn spaceship we ever put up there had faults. Every one of them had faults. When I worked for the U.S. Bureau of Mines, being a federally owned outfit, we were screened. We had to be investigated by the FBI to get a job there, some high priorities. Today, companies that make equipment for our spaceships, they don't even screen the employees that work there.

At least two months before the war, there was a meeting of all the high-rank military officials on Corregidor, and there was a Colonel Edison there who predicted the exact route that the Japs would take in attacking. But still there was never armament placed there that would or could have slowed them down, or at best defeat them.

We are a little bit prejudiced, of course, but we feel that if they had left the war in the Philippines up to the non-coms, what eventually happened to us would have never happened. It's just difficult to explain to anyone else and have them understand that these people, these Japs are just animals. The guards we had had no real reason for beating us, they just did so because we were taller than they. That just pissed them off, and made them feel superior when they beat on us. Because of what we experienced and because people don't accept or understand what we went through, they have a difficult time understanding or accepting us. Let me give you an example. When my mother died, I was standing at the coffin and I heard one of the people say, "Look, that Ken doesn't have a heart anymore. He isn't even having any remorse."

I turned and said, "When your body sees so much death, you don't have any tears in you anymore. There is nothing there to make a tear." But they didn't understand. Probably just thought I was crazy.

That is what happened to us. The only reason that we can communicate with each other so well, as former prisoners, is because we have the same thing in common. If four of us are sitting at a table talking, there is a lot of sharing. But if a stranger comes up, we would shut up right away. We just feel so misunderstood and unaccepted by others, and we've been made to feel that way since we returned home. People just can't believe what happened to us and thus can't understand us.

But I am a firm believer that the knowledge that we received has taught us that we could make anything go. There is nothing like "can't" in our vocabulary or dictionary. We will try anything. I am a good improviser. I think we learned something, I really do.

When I got home, I had about $4,000 in back pay waiting for me. But even in those times it went fast. In fact, the only real thing that I got out of the money was my wife's wedding and engagement rings. They cost around $800. I just blew the rest. I married a fine woman, and I have had a good life with her. She understands me better than I understand myself. That is the good thing that came out of this, for as a result, my life has been pleasant. I think my time over there led me to appreciate even more what I acquired when I got back over here.

I feel the guilt, too, but a lot of the good that happened to me overweighed some of the bad things. I try to push them to the back of my mind, and think of the good things.

Victor Mapes

In terms of pure drama, Victor Mapes' incarceration ranks with John Kennedy's and Papillon's. As a result of his continuous attempts to escape, he survived the experience with a minimum of emotional scars, considering the severity of his imprisonment. In fact, he admits to having learned some valuable and useful lessons from his imprisonment. "I know that I found out one thing for sure," he said. "I found out that hatred destroys. It can warp you and destroy you. Over there, I just tried to stay clear of it."

I was born in a little place called St. Cloud, which is near Disney World in central Florida. It is mostly a resort area now. We made our living largely by agriculture. My daddy was a dairyman and I loved the soil and everything that grows, and I was very active in the Boy Scouts. I was an Eagle Scout, and over a period of years, an assistant scout master.

I started working after I graduated from high school in 1938. It was Depression time yet, and I tried to get enough money to go to college. But war came fall of 1939. Hitler was on the rampage in Poland.

I was with a ROTC unit at college in Florida, and I got thinking and I said, "Oh, heck." And I went to see my girlfriend in Indiana during my college break and tell her I was thinking about joining the service, which I eventually did on the 8th of November, 1939, by enlisting in the Army Air Corps, Fort Ben, Harrison, Indiana.

From there we were shipped by train, and in pretty good style, to Fort Slocam, N.Y. Then we took our shots and in the winter we were shipped out of Brooklyn Army Base by Army transport, "Chateau Terrie," through the Panama Canal to Hickam Field, Honolulu, Hawaii, where I took my basic training. Right after that, I wanted to go to some sort of school. There were just so many people down there in the Army Air Corps. They had more men than they knew what to do with. After six months of schooling on detach service, Schofield Barracks, I got assigned to the 14th Bomb Squadron, B-18s. After a bit of time there, I was getting ready to be shipped back home when the War Department decided that I was going to be sent the other way—the Far East.

So under the cover of darkness, on the 3rd of September, 1941, we zigzagged clear across the Pacific Ocean. We were commanded by Captain O'Donald of West Point, who later became a three- or four-star general. We then landed at Manila under unsealed orders and found out that we were being sent to Clark Field, which was way up in the boondocks, somewhere in Pampanga Province, central Luzon. They had grassy air strips up there. We went up there by convoy. When we got there, the aborigines were running around. I heard there were pythons in the grass. It was a different way of life from in Hawaii.

The 14th Bomb Squadron was an elite outfit—high school graduates, some college graduates. So we adjusted quite well to that situation. We got paid double because they thought it was worth twice as much, but we only worked half a day, so that was considered a fat salary. During this time, a continuous military buildup was going on in the islands. You could see it going on daily.

On about 4:00 A.M. on the 8th of December, 1941, we got word that Pearl Harbor had just been bombed. And we couldn't believe it. Then we realized that the Japs would be soon coming for us over there. Our commanders couldn't make up their minds and got our butts in a bind. They weren't sure when to send our planes up and when not to. It appears that there was some sort of indecisiveness on General MacArthur's part. I later discovered that he had received orders from President Roosevelt not to fire until fired upon.

What we eventually did was to get our B-17s and B-18s airborne above Clark Field. Then at about noon they began to run out of gas and had to land. When they landed, they lined up in a straight row. I was in the mess hall at noon when I heard Don Bell broadcast over the radio that Clark Field is under attack. Hell, I was there and I didn't hear any bombs. So I went back up and looked up in the sky and I saw two formations of 27 bombers. Then all of a sudden it dawned on me, "Hell, those planes are Japs." Then I began to see the bombs fall. I jumped into an old bamboo-walled dugout. I grabbed this lieutenant's leg and tried to pull him in with me. He didn't know what was going on, and he cussed the hell out of me. "Get your hands off me, soldier," he said.

Then a bomb dropped right near him and he crawled in next to me. But we started choking because of all the smoke and dirt. The old gas masks didn't do any good. So we crawled out of there, as the Zeros attacked. We scrambled over next to a latrine, where I saw one of our guys take his shoe off and throw it, out of frustration, cussing, another firing his .45 pistol at a Zero passing by only about 50 feet overhead. Anyhow, I survived, but after that the Japs just swept clean the whole place with their air power and left it in shambles. Afterwards, I stayed at Clark Field helping to feed the hungry and wounded. I had four men with me at the time out and we vowed to stay together no matter what.

Then we went to the edge of the jungle where these pygmies stayed and where our troops, who had hid and survived, were. All our guys were trigger-happy. We had a very sleepless night and the mosquitoes bit us to death. Right then and there we decided to memorize each other's address in case any of us got out and we could get a hold of each other's people.

Bright and early the next morning we heard a pursuit plane try to take off. But his landing gear must have been hit or something because he just lost control, ran into a B-17, and then blew up. Things were very desperate there. Guys were willing to try anything to defend the base. The next few weeks the Japs just about annihilated us, bombing our nearby warehouses, planes, runways, everything, but we hung on and survived. Sometimes many raids a day. We just hung on there on the edge of that jungle. Then on December 24th we got word that the Japs landed nearby. They were moving against General Wainwright's troops. We were told that we had better get off Clark Field fast. So we retreated to a place called Bataan. Our commander, Captain O'Donald, told us to stockpile any edible food stuffs. We thought he was very conservative at the time, but he was right.

Shortly after the war started, I got drafted into the kitchen crew. On Christmas Eve we were sent with a truckload of food to Bataan, 90 miles. We had left some cooked roasts from a warehouse. When we got to Bataan before daylight the next morning, we almost got our heads shot off. Our guys there were scared and very trigger-happy. I fell asleep on some gravel while a hell of a battle waged. Corregidor was firing her massive guns at the Japs.

To show you how bad things were, we didn't have anything to cook in. So I went out scouting around in another Air Force outfit. I wanted to borrow a 5-gallon can to get some water. They gave me a hard time. They had some other things, but I could see they didn't have much food. So I went back and we opened up some cans of beef for us. Then I got some volunteers and we went clear back up to Clark Field on Christmas Day. When I left I had turned off the fire under our "field range" oven where the roast beef was being cooked for our Christmas dinner. But the guys couldn't wait for us to warm it up when we got back. They had decided to eat it cold.

On the 26th of December, 1941, we stayed on Bataan, and the Japs continued to bomb us. It was hell. The Japanese planes would fly right over us. It was nerve-wracking. But our outfit, the 19th Bomb group, was lucky.

Six hundred and some technicians got on an inter-island steamer that would hold about 200 people. When we got on that crowded ship, we had a hell of a run through the mine fields, until on 29 December 1941, and we finally got bombed off of Mindoro. I was a good swimmer but I got hit by shrapnel. They battened down the hatches of the holds, so we could not get below. I was caught topside. The Japs had already dropped three bombs and were coming around for another run. So I said, "I'm gonna get the hell off of here." So I dove the 30 feet into the water. I swam through a bunch of the boys and their equipment that they tossed overboard. Then the Japs dropped a fourth one between me and the ship. My impulse was to go underneath, but I stayed topside. But when that bomb hit nearby, it felt like it kicked me in the butt real good, like an old mule. Then I went searching around for men from my outfit. By the time I got back on our leaky ship, I had rescued six comrades struggling in deep water.

We rendezvoused and ended up on Mindoro somewhere around New Year's 1942, and later landed at the DelMonte Plantation. We then got organized and took off, rendezvousing not far from DelMonte air strip, called the "Suicide Strip." There was a whole bunch of us, 600 technicians and about a thousand other people nearby. We watched the Japs bomb the plantation and everything. But they never did detect us in these little coffee bean trees about six feet high. From there, we were taken out to meet up with others of my outfit in February 1942. And there we ran into some of the strange-looking people that I had read about before. They were Moros. They were different from the Christian Filipinos, and they wore turbans and they looked like what you would see in old biblical days. We soon found out they were shrewd traders and they weren't to be trusted. But since the Japanese hit they tolerated us more than they would have otherwise.

So our mission was to hold the airstrip open in case our planes would come back up there. We stayed around there with the Moros, living off the land as best we could. Then the rumors went from bad to worse. About April we also built a sea plane base and had it ready, and we had one of those PT boats salvaged from the navy. We were under General Sharp. We were pretty much self-sufficient. Finally we got the word that some nurses and brass were coming down at last from the last hold out on Corregidor. These two PBY planeloads of nurses came in and we did everything we could to make them feel comfortable with our fried bananas, home-ground strong coffee, and rice. But when they landed, all that they wanted to do at first was go to the latrine. So the captain had to chase the few guys who didn't go down to the beach for their landing away from their crude slit-trench primitive latrines.

One of the PBYs hit an obstruction and damaged a pontoon on the way in. So they planned to fly out with some nurses after dark to Australia.

The other half of the nurses there were taken to the DelMonte strip to go out. These were taken prisoners later.

We were a pitiful looking bunch. Many didn't have any shoes or much else. So the commanders told the nurses that if they had anything they felt we could use to leave it behind. They gave us some guns and whatever they could. The pilots knew that it was going to be a long flight for them, and they also wanted to lighten their load. Some of the boys came back with bras on and everything. The PBY just got off before a Jap plane arrived in the late evening. It took them quite a while, though, 'cause one of our guys had tried to stow away on board and they couldn't get up enough steam to get over the tree line. But the pilots finally figured out what was going on, found the guy and threw him out of his hiding place to balance the plane.

After that, Gen. Royce of Australia decided to make one more big bombing run, and they bombed all the way up to Clark Field. That is when the Japs, in retaliation, really went after us because we were at large on Mindanao. Corregidor fell on the 10th of May and we were still at large. We didn't surrender until the 27th of May, 1942. We were in a mountain holdout, General G. O. Fort's 81st P H & L Army Division. We had the Moros below us as a buffer zone. I think we could have held out. But we were ordered to surrender. I argued with the order, telling superiors that I would rather take my chances in the hills, but I was told that I would be classified as the last active enemy and a deserter. I then would lose all my privileges as an American citizen. So I decided to go on into the prison camp, then try to escape later. My philosophy was that anybody that was captured was like a chicken with his head cut off. How is he going to give you orders? And that was the position that Gen. Wainwright, who had already surrendered, was in. And most of all, the people on Mindanao believed what Wainwright said through the Japs. That is the gospel truth. I talked to a lot of people. It was a real sore thing with me. Then when I came back to the states I talked to the Navy at Annapolis. One thing they wanted to know about was believing in someone else in an unconditional surrender. But I wouldn't let myself be talked into answering their questions. I would have just been made out to look either dumb or a coward, neither of which I was. But I now understand how everything happened. MacArthur ducked out to Australia. That was a low blow. We felt like we were deserted. The whole thing was just a downhill drag. So he left Wainwright to do his surrendering for him. But anyway, we got caught in this crap.

We were still in pretty good shape on Mindanao. But most all the other boys in PI had taken a heck of a blasting. Anyway, I saw the whole thing in PI [the Philippine Islands] go down the drain and I surrendered, reluctant with it, with about 50 of us Americans and 300 Filipinos, 27 May 1942. The Moros got pretty bad at that time. They killed some of our guys and stole from them. Then we had to contend with the Japs and the disease and the jungle.

Anyhow, we were interned at Camp Keepley, Mindanao. Soon after that, I felt I was capable of escaping, and living as good as anyone out in the jungle and such, and take my chances. What I calculated was we might make a mass escape—so many men might make it. But a few guys in our outfit jumped the gun and thus the Japs found out, and then they got really mean. They took out a West Point colonel, Colonel Vesey, and Captain Price, who was an artillery officer who had blasted Japs quite a bit, and my first sergeant, Charlie Chandler, and they took them out and shot them. We never saw them again, but I always remember them. Then the Japs decided to take us out and shoot every one of us. Then our commander, Colonel Mitchell, begged the Japs to give us at least a fighting chance. The Japs had machine guns aimed. They were serious, but upon Mitchell's request, they decided to give us at least a fighting chance by putting us on a Death March.

So there were two or three Filipinos that warned us not to take any chances. "They will kill you," they told us. This was the first thing that we had heard about the Jap's Death March techniques. So we started out, wired together, and we had to go 42 kilometers in one day. But it was mostly downhill and we were in fair shape, so were the Filipinos, barefooted and everything. We hadn't gone very far when we lost our first man. He was a civilian named Childers. They executed him. The Jap that executed him kind of liked me. He was a wrestler and he had a beard, and so did I. He wanted me to take the dead man's tobacco and peanut brittle.

Then this Major Nevin who was in front of me started staggering and finally fell out and I bent over him and tried to talk him into coming to. But he said he couldn't make it anymore. I asked the nearby medic if he could help him. He just stared. The Japs just shot Nevin right there, and he kicked like an animal who had got his head cut off. I'll never forget that. Blood spurting out all over and everything. They shot him in the head and chest. They stabbed him with a bayonet just for good measure. Later on, they killed some Filipinos too. Later that night, we stayed in a school house.

What the Jap idea was, was to march us as far as they could. That way nobody would be left alive. But what happened was that we changed commands at Illigan so the Japs would come out looking like winners and wouldn't have to lose face. Some of our older men would have never made it much more than one day if we hadn't changed guards at Illigan after 42 kilometers. Then they just put us on a troop ship, Tito Marue, and shipped us out to Malaybalay Prison Camp. We went ashore and up to where the Filipino Army had been stationed before the war in central Mindanao. We were under General Sharp. We were real "fat cats" down there. The Japs there felt that since American soldiers gave up all our food and everything and surrendered, that we could be trusted. So they treated us more like guests, and they had us do one thing or another. But then water and food was getting short and two Filipinos took off. Then they caught them, brought them back, tied them to a post and shot them right in front of us just to make an impression so we wouldn't try the same thing. I will always remember those two guys just hanging there. After that, the Japs got real mean.

They would shake you down and torture you. They would come up and try to kick you in the testicles. I still have scars on my hip. They were always slapping at you. They would haul off and hit you for no reason at all.

I figured that I stood a better chance of staying in PI and escaping than if I got sent off to Japan. So when they interrogated me, I fed them a lot of lies about my background so they wouldn't want me.

Any guy that even said he knew how to drive a Model-T, the Japs took him. The POWs thought they were going to get jobs driving trucks, but they simply took anybody that professed any technical knowledge and took them over to Japan. They then left a bunch of us guys behind. Then they took off in October 1942 and went to Manila on a prisoner-of-war boat and then on up to Japan. And most of them ended up in steel mills in Kawasaki, but they didn't get to drive any trucks. They just pushed coal carts in the mine or something. They stayed there until after the A-bomb was dropped.

We, instead, went south to a penal colony, Davoo [Dapecol], where Filipinos had kept their incorrigibles. It was something like Devil's Island. On the way down to Davoo penal colony [Camp II], I was in the back end of the truck and it was all crowded. I said to myself, "I don't like the looks of this place. It looks too much like Devil's Island."

Just then this Jap guard next to me turned and said, "You know why you are being sent here, don't you?" He could speak English.

I said, "Why?"

He said, "Because you killed Japs."

Right then and there I made up my mind to get the hell out of there. I was real jittery.

Finally, they needed a volunteer to work on a sawmill detail right after I got there, and I went on that. It was to a place on the coast of Mindanao. I stayed there until after Christmas 1942 or somewhere after the first of the year 1943, and I did pretty good. I always told the Filipinos I was hungry and I would fill my scrap lumber cart so loaded that the Jap guard would have to call some Filipinos in to push, and they'd sneak me some chow and I'd bury it in the sawdust to eat later. But the Japs started getting wise to what I was doing because I wasn't losing any weight like other POWs. So they sent me back to the main camp after a few weeks. After I returned to the main camp, I worked a year in rice paddies. Later in August 1944, while on detail in Lasang, I was laying there and I heard this noise and I said, "Boy, this is an American plane." The American pilot came over high, then he cut his motor and bombed the airstrip three or four times. The bombs fell only about a quarter of a mile from where the POWs were fenced in at the Lasang airstrip. From then on, they put us on half rations and guarded us closely. Shortly after, they put us on a prison ship, No. 84, and we were attacked at Davao Harbor. We sailed down to Davao Gulf and we spent ten days anchored in a harbor and holed up in the hot bottom of the POW ship. The Japs were trying to dodge all our lurking submarines. Then they got real brave and went up the Zamboango coast. We traveled at night and stayed hidden in daytime. We got up to a place called Sindangan Point. And they got real brave with their seven-ship convoy. They started across the large bay instead of hugging the coast, and they didn't know that our coastwatchers there had alerted the U.S. sub, Paddle, about four o'clock in the evening, 6 September 1942, while we were in the hot hole. The U.S. sub, Paddle, threw two "tin fish" into our prison ship, Shinyo Maru, with 750 American POWs in it. I protected myself the best I could by getting into the ballast of the ship, where there was a four-foot pipe going from the bottom to the top. So I bent down there and there was this priest, Father LaFleur, praying beside me. That was the last I remember. When I came to, the water was about eight or ten feet above my head. I realized I could still move a little, and I started crawling up the pipe like a drowned rat. When I got my head just above the water, I could see that the ship was sinking fast. Topside, I could see most of the men had already got out. I then slid out through a crack in the ship as the thing lurched and I slid across the deck, sinking. I got to the hatch cover going out into the open sea. There was a bunch of Jap soldiers nearby in a lifeboat and they shot at me but they hit somebody else. But that time, the Shinyo Maru POW boat had begun to capsize. It took about eight minutes to capsize. As it went down it started sucking us back toward it, but it didn't pull far enough back to drown us, thank God. The old ship kept blowing its whistle like a bellowing wounded bull until it went down out of sight. Then it was nothing but bubbles, and much quieter. There were about 25 people on the hatch cover. They were maimed and moaning and everything. There was a Captain Cleveland there who took his belt and my g-string and made a splint for the broken bones in my right leg, past the lower and upper portions, both bones of which were sticking out in plain view, bleeding and very painful.

What happened was the U.S. submarine, Paddle, had hit four of the seven Jap ships in the convoy. But we were in the only one that was a prison ship. Some of the other damaged Jap ships were grounded, though, and Japs were shooting at us from these grounded ships. I seen what they were up to. They were expecting none of us to survive. I swam away with this splint on my right leg, and I saw one of my old buddies, Mike Pulucie, there and he had a bad leg, too.

I said to him, "We will make it together. Together, we'll have at least two good legs." Our luck, he had the same leg busted as I did, but he had half of a life preserver to hold. We then ran into this old U.S. doctor, Colonel Culver, and asked him to come along with us, with our two bad legs and all. But he decided instead to go back and try to help some guys on a raft. Some sort of projectile hit the raft, though. They obliterated the raft and him, too.

They shot at me until nightfall. I was holding onto a saki box, but I couldn't navigate the damn box out there. So I let loose and tried to catch onto a timber. There was a five-mile current and I felt I couldn't catch it, but I could see that the current was going in a semi-circle so I swam straight across and got to the timber. I hung onto it for dear life until about midnight. And then here came one of those damn Jap launches, chugging. I don't know whether they were looking for me or not. But I wasn't taking any chances because they headed right for me. So I snuggled down behind that timber and they saw the timber. In fact, the Jap at the bow of the boat was so close that I could see him silhouetted against the moon. His craft went one way and then the timber went the other way, and there I was, all alone in the deep water in the dark, but he didn't see me. I was there that way a while, praying. I couldn't find anything to hold onto and I could hear dogs bark on the beach, though, which was about two miles away or so, and there was a light high up on the hill. A star had finally come out. Anyhow, I got awfully thirsty. The only water I had was from a canteen I had taken off a shell-shocked Jap guard. I ran across a part of a palm leaf and stuck the branch-like stem part in my mouth. It soon started to rain and I was able to catch some water that way for my terrible thirst.

Then I ran into a big oil slick out there. It got in my beard and covered me. I was afraid it was going to catch on fire because there was still smoke and everything all around. Then about 3:00 A.M., I ran across a board that was about 30 feet long and two feet wide. So I grabbed that board. It was nailed together on two sides. Later the sun came up and about 10:30 A.M. or so, the fog lifted. By that time I saw a little native boat out there. I yelled at it. I suppose he was about a half-mile away. But he was going the other way fast and didn't hear me. I didn't know where the hell I was at but I knew I was getting closer and closer to shore—"Green water ahead!"

Finally, I approached land at about eleven o'clock, 7 September 1944, and a bunch of natives, dressed in burlap sacks, came out in an outrigger canoe to meet me as I was caught in the breakers. They picked me up, pulled me over into the outrigger and gave me a T-shirt full of holes, a raw banana and a raw egg. When we landed on the beach, Japs started shooting at us from a sea plane all around, and I thought the natives were going to leave me right there or turn me back in to the Japs. But they hurriedly took me along with the outrigger to hide under a big tree. So they got me underneath the tree there, and one of them had a new short rifle. I had never seen a gun like that. He let me look at it. It had the number 43 rifle shells. The guy with the gun could speak English and he told me that he had gotten the gun off a U.S. submarine that had come in. He was the only one that could speak English out of the group. He said he had been a trainer, a Filipino scout. So then they took me to an old native house and gave me water, by spoonfuls. I was crazy for water.

Then they gave me some cornmeal chicken gruel. At night they moved me down the beach to another place. There was another guy there, an American who had had amnesia, and he had just come to. He was a non-com named Bill Lorton.

The Japs came in that night and the natives left us alone in a house on the beach. The Japs came in and raided the place but they didn't find us. The next day, we went up 60 kilometers in outriggers to another place up the coast where all those that survived, the 80 out of the original 250, were being taken. It was called Sindangau Bay. A few weeks later a submarine from Australia, Narwhal, came in and got us. It took three nights to get in, but they finally made it. Got all of us aboard. It was a huge thing, looked as big as a battleship to me. It was 362 foot long with two six-inch guns on deck.

I was one of the first ones out there, too. For by that time my painful, swollen leg was all gangrened and foul-smelling. I didn't have much longer to live unless I got help. I'd made it three weeks with it that way already. So I was made "priority one" to leave by Col. H. MacGee.

After the sub, Narwhal, popped up for the third time, they sent a party ashore to get us. And the first fellow I saw was this great big blond guy. As he approached me with a dinghy, he looked like a monster, he was so big.

The first thing he said to me was, "I am so glad to see you."

And I said, "Not half as glad as I am to see you. Let's get the hell out of here. Now!"

But then he said, "Wait a minute, I have something to do."

I thought he was going to do his business or something. But instead of that, he got out and walked a ways down through the sand and wiggled his feet. Then he said, "Boy, does that feel good. I haven't felt sand for months."

I said, "Let's get out of here. Quick."

So we started out in the dinghy and the natives' outriggers were passing us like mad and here we were in this little dinghy, paddling along real slow. And I wanted to get out of there. Hell, I thought that with my luck the sub would leave before we got there.

Finally I asked, "Do you have a tow rope?" and he nodded.

Then I said, "I'll tell you what. When one of those fast outriggers comes by here, we'll yell and see if we can get us a tow."

So we caught one that was going out and he gave us a tug. He didn't worry about us. He was just going out there to see the sub. I got out there about 15 minutes before anybody else.

Then the guys on the sub didn't know what to do with me. They didn't know whether they should put me in through the connine tower or the torpedo tube. But they finally got me in and put me in traction. The next five days we spent going south in dangerous enemy waters until we finally arrived safe in Dutch New Guinea. They had a doctor on board the sub. But he was useless as far as helping me out; he was so seasick all the time. I was lucky; I hit a Navy field hospital when we landed at Mios Wendl Island, Dutch New Guinea. They had a good commander there and they gave me penicillin, which I had never heard of at the time, and a direct blood transfusion and ice packs. I had a fever of about 105°. They saved my life. It took two years to get my leg mended at Walter Reed Hospital. Then it finally broke in two again, so I had to get a pediograph. I finally retired as a master sergeant several years later after 22 years in the service. When the sub picked me up on September 27, 1944, I weighed less than 100 pounds. I finally got back in the States on December 10, 1944, five years to the day after I had left in 1939.

I survived all that I did because I feel that I had a different philosophy than some others. A psychiatrist at Walter Reed Hospital verified that for me; that's why he thought I made it. He said, "You have a different philosophy." I always felt that something, no matter how little, was better than nothing.

I know that I found out one thing for sure. I found out that hatred destroys. It can warp you and destroy you. Over there, I just tried to stay clear of it.

I'll tell you one thing that I found out for sure, Americans are stupid in one way. They don't realize that whenever you deal with the Japanese that they are going to get the best end of the bargain. If you don't think so, just look around. It is happening right now. You might figure you are getting a good bargain, but they are going to get one better. The American people don't understand that. Right now, the Japs are taking over things without firing a shot.

What I did to survive, though, was religious to a certain extent. I took religion pretty seriously, and in the long run you have to use all your resources. We were so close to death all the time, we couldn't worry about things. When we went to bed at night we didn't know whether the Japs were going to kill us or not. One thing that hurt me more than anything else, though, and that was watching my perfectly good body go to hell. I had sores all over me and I was all diseased up. I had rotten teeth and I couldn't see too well. My eyes were going. I did the best I could to keep myself clean and everything. But still, to see your body shrivel up and to see what is happening to the other people, that was hard to take.

But I just kept praying that I could still have a good mind. That was the main thing for me. My body was going to hell, but I kept my good mind. That is how I made it. It was that kind of philosophy that kept me alive. I also tried not to worry myself sicker. Some guys worried themselves to death. I guess you can understand. But I just figured that if I kept a strong mind, that that would be the key to my survival, a strong open mind.

Coming back home presented some difficulties though, too. Learning to be a free man again and accepting that was a challenge. For a whole year I never set foot in a bar or a movie for long because I couldn't sit still. I didn't know what it was to just be calm, to be relaxed. I was all hyped up.

Later on, I got reassigned to an air base in Hokkaido, which is in northern Japan, near the Russian border. I was assigned to an NIOIC training center. They had some ex-Jap soldiers working there, and they used to be sent down to me at the end of each afternoon after they'd run out of things to do. So I'd tell them to fix this or fix that.

Then one day, I just happened to see a Jap coming toward me and I remembered seeing him on the dikes in Mindanao. So I got all shook up and I came right up to him and I said, "I know who you are. You were one of the guards back when I was working the carabou rice paddies during World War II in Mindanao."

And he got all shook up and just took off. But he had never bothered me. He had been a good guard, but it took me three weeks to get him back to finish painting the door he was working on when I ran into him. That is the only Jap guard I ever saw that I had remembered seeing as a POW. Then another thing I was scared of by going back over to Japan was that a friend of mine killed a Jap over there and he got in a lot of trouble.

I had 17 Japs working for me, and what I told them was, "Look, I have been a prisoner of war over here, and I was roughed up so I know what it is like. But I'll tell you what I'll do. I'll give you a fair deal. I won't take advantage of you." And I never had a bit of trouble with them.

I can't believe how these people could regiment themselves from one extreme to another. You just can't believe it. These fellows can be so belligerent and then so otherwise. But they are pretty much all alike. What I mean by that is that because of the fact that as a race they have been isolated for so long, that they all have pretty similar beliefs and ideas.

What we have here in the United States is a mixed podge of people. We have a melting pot. But their oneness as a people, I think that is the secret of their success as a people. They are way ahead of us in some ways.

But one thing that kept us alive, which was different from the Japs, was that if we can't do it one way, we'll do it another. Our sense of humor is admirable as well. I know mine helped to keep me alive.

PART TWO

THE BATTLE OF THE BULGE

More American troops were captured (23,554) during the Battle of the Bulge than during any other U.S. engagement of any war. At this concluding stage of the war, Germany barely had food for its citizens, let alone the captured soldiers of enemy nations. A tremendous resentment had also grown within the German people for the soldiers of their invading enemies. Yet occasional displays of tremendous compassion by individual Germans, as seen in the following pages, still took place.

Charles Stenger

Charles Stenger put his experience as a POW to direct and complete use in his life. His insights and efforts have enabled many former POWs to live comfortably with their past.

I was just going to try to tell you a little about my POW experience. Before the service, I was a small kid and simply never saw myself as a macho person. I ran track, played football, and so on, but I did not have a real macho kind of self-image. The thing that happened when I was captured, and in somehow surviving all these terrible experiences, I began to realize that I had more inner strength than I realized. However, the guys who thought they were macho, the "Let's beat the hell out of those Germans" type, for them it was a traumatic letdown. They found out they were tremendously vulnerable and simply could not continue to cope in an aggressive style as before without risking injury or death. But what surprised me was that I found out that I was stronger.

I was an extremely important person because I was a medic, and there's no more important person in such a situation as war as a medic. I did all the gory things that you read about or hear about a medic doing in wartime. So my self-esteem did not deteriorate like the others' did. But for most, they became depressed. They realized they were ineffective and powerless, at the whim of the guards, as they saw it. In contrast, I never felt helpless. I had a role still, a personality, an identity. I kept just saying to myself over and over, "I am not a prisoner of war." I was even bold enough to rattle the camp gates from time to time and order the guard to let me out, which he would do, if you had an assertive attitude. The important thing for me was that I had a role in the prison camp. I was important because I took care of people, whereas the other prisoners were exploited, beaten, and so on. So their experience was destructive to their sense of self-worth.

As a result, I came back, and despite all the blood and gory details, I never even had a nightmare. I think this is in part due to the fact that I went into the entire experience realizing that this is a very dangerous world. But for so many others the opposite was the case, and the sudden loss of self, loss of identity either injured their psyches permanently or killed them.

That was the key to surviving as a POW in World War II, and to being able to live with yourself afterward: not being so damaged by the experience that you couldn't leave it behind. And to be able to personally do that, one had to be capable of retaining their sense of self-worth, even after their identity, all that they associated their selves with being was stripped away. It's the same with any difficult situation—a death, a loss of job, and so on—that an individual goes through. Such is also the reason some recover from such events and some don't. It's best not to too fully associate oneself with something that can be taken away from you—a job, a person, an identity, whatever. For if that is taken away from you, you go down for good. Real self-esteem has nothing to do with one's actual identity, that is, being a POW, but with how one really sees themselves, no matter what the outside world sees or projects upon them.

As a result of my mindset, being a POW actually became a positive experience for me. Being an adult means that you are in charge of your own life. When you are a prisoner of war, you are not in charge of anything. You can not even say you are going to go to the john or anything. So once one's sense of competence, one's hope is eroded, they start to give up, to die. But thank God that did not happen with me.

In 1971–72, I headed the VA committee to prepare the VA system for returning Vietnam veterans, a brand new division for us, and our first attempt at helping these combat veterans in general. They were coming back with a very angry attitude. They were ungrateful. They had long hair. They didn't give a damn for authority. As a result, since they returned, they were alienated. It was very obvious that many were sick yet wouldn't stay in the hospitals. They were more likely to leave against medical advice. If they weren't treated in a certain way that they were comfortable with, they would become unruly. You had to establish some degree of rapport with them. So this committee that I headed for the VA, which included social workers, Vietnam veterans, and so on, developed theories and criteria on how to deal with the Vietnam veteran.

To begin, we developed a typical profile of a Vietnam veteran. The head administrator at the time had a son in Vietnam and was very responsive to this. Donald Johnson was his name. He eventually got a very bad name later for dealing with Vietnam veterans. But it wasn't his fault. He simply got trapped in something and he didn't handle it well. At any rate, the first Vietnam veterans to go against the war made a statement by marching on Washington when the VA was to hold its first seminar on the problematic dilemma of the Vietnam veteran. We brought in people from hospitals all around the D.C. area and the East to learn about Vietnam veterans. Once they learned of the marchers' intentions, almost all the administrator's staff wanted to cancel our meeting. But I insisted that this was just a perfect time to go ahead. The head administrator agreed, even though he knew that the Vietnam vets would force an incursion on our VA hospital. But instead of being inconvenienced by it, we prepared for it; and when they came to force their incursion, we just invited them in to be part of the program, and it worked beautifully. It was a good eye-opener. But the prevailing attitude in our society, and as well as in VA at the time, was, "What the hell are these guys coming back being angry at us, wearing long hair and looking dirty?" Such was the generalized anger and hostility dealing with and to which the vets were reacting. Ideally, you want your soldiers to come back from the war the same way they did in World War II and Korea, proud and happy. But the Vietnam vets didn't come back that way. So this created a problem. Society blamed the victim: "They weren't good soldiers like we were."

Now, as psychologists, we knew that that wasn't the case. So what we did on this committee was to develop guidelines to deal with the situations and the victims. We had to set up a little Vietnam center in each hospital so the veterans could at least get together. Then when a Vietnam vet was released, we made it quite clear and set up specific guidelines so that a vet could go to any VA hospital and get counseling or whatever he needed.

All this brought me in touch with the Vietnam POW as well, which is a situation no one fully understands unless you have been through it and recognized what was happening and learned from it. For what happens when you suddenly become a prisoner of war, with no training in how to deal with such, is that you go into a state of shock. You cannot believe something like this is happening to you. You are both scared to death and have a total sense of disbelief. But what you learn immediately is that if you don't do exactly what you are told, you will be killed. So you quickly learn to comply, which contributes to a continuing sense of fear that at any moment you can be killed or injured. You see that happening to people all around you. They tested the guards too much, and were hit in the head with a rifle, shot, beat, or whatever. All this happens when you are feeling so damned helpless and useless. One of the ways that you can try to regain a little bit of self-esteem is to test the limits, like kids testing the limits of their parents. We would test the limits that we could put on the guards. In other words, if we got them angry we wouldn't feel so powerless. Kids do the same thing with their parents. We did exactly the same thing. Sometimes we tested too far, almost provoking the guards.

I don't know if you ever watched "Hogan's Heroes," you know, the TV series. But we did many of the things they did on the show. They were crazy, but we did them nonetheless. That program was not particularly well received by prisoners of war because it didn't show the other side, the deprivation. But it did show many of the crazy things that happened in most POW camps by the POWs just trying to force the guards to be angry or something like that. It is true that if you get somebody angry, that you at least have got to be worth something, or they wouldn't pay any attention to you at all.

It is important to realize that when you are a prisoner of war you have to adapt to it, and it's easier for one to do so if one doesn't see the guards as always an immediate threat. You do try to see them in friendly ways. So we developed pet names for the different guards. Some of the guards were not hostile. Then, there were some guards that were hostile. But most seemed like half-way decent people. They are caught in a situation just like you are. The more that we could see them as non-threatening, the less angry we got. So that there was not a tendency to carry that anger along with you during that time and later after you left. But most prisoners coming back describe their situations as terrible. They show a lot of angry emotion about their enemy, kind of an emotional hangover from the war. Even though they were free, the memory stays with them, and it is hard for them to feel free of the fact that they can again hurt you, or that someone can, ever again the way you were hurt before. So you tend to have not a dispassionate attitude. I personally really feel no hostility about that situation today, even though I knew they starved us unnecessarily and didn't help those they could have. But I don't feel hostility about it. I kind of say to myself, "Well, Jesus, here their country was being blown up all around them, this city, that city was being bombed two or three times a day. How would you expect them to feel?"

But prisoners of war in general do have a deep-rooted anger about them. They will talk about the Japanese and the Korean guards in very angry, incomplete ways, and they don't do it with a lot of emotion. But they may show that emotion about other things. They are still holding onto their feelings to some degree. For they learned to survive by not letting themselves feel. For feeling can get you in trouble, like, "I am going to knock that guy's block off." That could get you killed. So you learn not to let yourself experience emotion that would help you to lose control of yourself, and it works very well.

On the Death March, which was the cruelest of all treatments received by our POWs, survival meant doing nothing, just continuing to walk and try to find your way while those around you are butchered. You may feel that hatred, but you are not in any position to act on it. There just is no way you can. So the feelings that "these sons of bitches aren't going to kill me," or "I am not going to do them a favor and die," that was certainly true. But it takes different forms once that feeling is internalized. They don't act on it. They can't. They'll be killed. Thus, they would not permit themselves any emotion that would challenge their guards, because on the Death March they would be beheaded, stabbed immediately, whatever.

But I don't recall feeling that when I was crossing Germany as a POW. I just felt, "God, when is this damn thing going to get over?" I kind of saw all of us as caught up, the guards, everyone, in this one lousy situation. We are there because we are there, that's all. Some of the guards were brutal, but some of the American soldiers could be very brutal as well. So these are the extremes on the range of human responses.

Most gentlemen came into the service with an already formed identity, being macho, or this or that, the standard male attitude. And after the POW experience, they spend the rest of their lives trying to recover that feeling.

In military training you are trained to feel that way as well. You feel macho. You do macho things. There is a common thread amongst all POWs and hostages: They lose control over their lives, and thus lose their identities, and they spend the rest of their time after their release trying to recover it. Such was the case with the hostages in Iran. All of a sudden they had absolutely no control over anything. Most of us have grown up, been trained, to feel effective in coping with life and all of a sudden, all our sense of self, which is based on perceiving ourself as able to function, whether it is write books or whatever the hell it is, is gone. We feel some degree of effectiveness. All of a sudden all removed from you. And in its place is a tremendous sense of ineffectiveness and helplessness to cope with anything. This, combined with the fear and the starvation and the things that went with it, certainly took most to the deepest points of ineffectiveness as a person. That is the most destructive thing associated with being a POW, that ineffectiveness as a person.

The psychological goal of a former prisoner of war is somehow to find a way to return to that sense of self, your importance as an individual. For when one is a prisoner, one prisoner is interchangeable with another. You are like rats. It doesn't really matter who you are since you have no importance as an individual to the enemy anyway. You may have importance as a symbol of their fear. You have no personal value to them, and you find that out very quickly. Because if you die, you die, and no one cares. So the most destructive impact is to your sense of self-worth.

The fear, the danger, and all that is probably similar to the combat situation. But in combat, of course, you at least can do something about your situation. You can shoot or something. You usually are busy. You don't have a chance to think about it. But as a POW you are helpless to cope with anything. You are totally under the control of other people who just don't give a damn about you, and that is a new experience for most of us.

Most of us grew up in situations as kids under feeling that people loved and cared about us. All of a sudden you find yourself in a war where that doesn't exist anymore, you just don't have any value whatsoever. That is the problem that persists in many prisoners of war—the post-traumatic stress syndrome. You have the fear and all that, the shattering or the erosion of your self-esteem. A lot of them continue to need some interaction with each other, almost to share stories of how they survived to restore temporarily their sense of self-esteem, and of course it does work. The same happens in the American Legion, the VFW, whatever. They go and tell their war stories.

At any rate, myself, when I got back, I had no contact with prisoners-of-war community. I didn't even know it existed. I just went back and started up where my life had left off, ably working with prisoners of war in the Veterans Administration. Then heading the efforts in that area and after my work with the Vietnam veterans, I became conscious of this as a special problem. For I had solved the problem for myself by repressing it successfully. But when I started working with the VA and planning for the returning Vietnam prisoners of war, I realized we didn't know a damn thing about our prisoners of war from other conflicts, even the numbers involved. So I got very actively involved in researching and writing some papers on the subject and making a lot of speeches. That's when the national POW organization became aware of what I was doing. When I retired they nailed me fast to be their advocate, to speak in their behalf, and that is what I have done on an unpaid basis from 1980 to the present. I have written most of the legislation on the POW experience and testified before Congress and such. I have also done a lot of work with veterans' appeals, for guys whose records were lost and couldn't get any benefits, and now were in bad shape. I did that for the last ten years, focusing on helping the POW whose war ailments and injuries are either just surfacing or being recognized now. And while you fail many times, you succeed sometimes, so the guys who really deserve the help from the Veterans Administration really get it. The main thing that we got was that we got the VA to admit that POWs routinely had more medical and psychological problems than the average vet. But it took until the early '80s to get any response. Yet at least now, if you are a former POW, you can just come and be admitted for anything in any VA hospital in the country. The VA now is very tuned in to prisoners of war, in terms of the health care and psychological care. The disability compensation side, we're still fighting like hell for that. No one can go through the stress, the starvation, and so on that these guys went through, as any health professional will tell you, and not suffer from some severe mental and physical after effects.

While with the VA, I did renewed relevant research comparisons. For example, if you take rats—wild rats—and put them through some of the same experiences of being captured and under total control, and these wild rats when you have them under total control, they don't even bite you. Their blood pressure goes down and their heart maybe goes down, and they die. You could just hold them in your hands. It was quite interesting. Such is called the survival instinct. You had to develop a survival instinct to stay alive as a POW.

As a POW, it doesn't matter whether you have been captured for one day or ten years. The one thing that you share with other captives is a sudden experience of being totally helpless, and that is a one-time, strong traumatic impact. The rest of the work from that time on is coping with the situation. But the sudden terrible thought that you are in control of absolutely nothing, and you are helpless in the face of people that don't give a damn whether you lived or died, is traumatizing. All prisoners and all hostages, of any type, share that. The differences between them is really in what happens afterward.

In the Korean and the Japanese prison camps, the threat was more immediate and visible, of course. But prisoners of the Germans felt that threat as well. It was an implied threat, but it hurt people nonetheless because it still reinforced that feeling within them. After a while, you just kind of get numb to these things.

It didn't matter whether one died or 100 died around you. The main difference between POWs occurs as the result of the length of time one had as a POW, which directly leads to the erosion of one's self-confidence. You can reach a point where you just give up. When that happened, a POW usually died within a few days.

The real tragedy, though, is that most of these men have had to go 40 years without treatment. You can see that, as a culture, we can see how if an individual goes through a traumatic experience, that he needs to work through his feelings in regard to that experience as soon as possible. If a high school kid or a grade school kid gets killed, counselors come to that school and help the others with it as soon as possible. Certainly, it should have been the same thing here. Anyone that went through combat or the prisoner-of-war experience needed and should have had that kind of help. But the great American myth was at the time, "We can take it, and when it is over it is over." For example, when you saw the Vietnam prisoners getting off those planes, I don't know whether you remember it or not, but they were saluting and the band was playing, and they look good. There is kind of a tendency to feel like, "By God, they did it," and there is no sense that they are in need of help. That is a tragedy. It is called the second injury: Everyone now treats them as normal. That really is a tragedy because these guys did generally feel somewhat embarrassed about being captured. And there is a little bit of feeling that maybe people won't be proud of them because of that, although that really is not true. For all the surveys have shown that they are held in high esteem. The American public is compassionate towards anyone that has been a prisoner of war. They feel they know what they went through. But the guys do tend to feel displaced, ashamed. It goes with a sense of loss of self-esteem that persists. They feel that somehow they aren't quite worthy. They just don't talk about it. Why tell people when you have failed?

They seal up that part of their life. Prisoners of war traditionally don't tell their families anything about it. I never did. I don't remember telling anyone. You may mention a few of the experiences but you don't mention the impact of it. So most just kept those feelings inside themselves and tried to get back and make it. In fact, they would make it, in most cases, at a lower level. They would function in society, get married, and all that. And that's one of the most amazing things about prisoners of war: Their wives, in almost every case, and I don't know how they were selected like this, are almost always a tremendous support system. They almost all talk about their wives and how wonderful they have been. I think this happens in part because the wife in the marriage is now feeling a huge amount of self-esteem because she has to be a stronger person for her husband. The wives are absolutely tremendous. There are very few of them that have deserted their guys. They have done the job the government should have done, of being someone that their husbands could lean on.

But yet prisoners of war have just suppressed all these feelings about their experiences and continue to do so except with their buddies from the war. But as they have grown older, as their physical strength and other things have started to diminish a bit, these past experiences begin to creep out and anxiety results. The problems that were never resolved start to come to the surface. So that now the guy experiences even more extremely the nightmares of his POW experiences. The outsider thinks, "Jesus, that happened years ago." It is very hard for the average person to understand that. But the point is that the POW has fielded it off for 30 or 40 years, when he was busy directing his energies and diluting his anxieties. He didn't have the strength to face it. He is now overwhelmed by those kinds of feelings. There is no question that as the prisoners of war get older, I don't want to use the words "fall apart," but they definitely start to show many of the post-traumatic symptoms. It is also true of the combat veterans. As they age they also will go though—not everyone obviously, but many of them—will go through this kind of resurgence of the anxiety. And some of those feelings, and this is the first that this generation, so to speak, of health givers realize that those kind of feelings do persist and exist.

There simply was no understanding that such would ever happen and the prisoners of war themselves were not helpful because they went back to their individual lives. They just tried to forget their experiences and get back to living. They are the least complaining group of veterans that we have. They just never complained about anything. You can see why. When you have been starving and brutalized, you are so damn grateful to be free again. You have nothing to complain about. They believed that the government, the VA would take care of them. Yet most POWs made it on their own. Now the problem is the reverse of what the VA has experienced with veterans as a whole. Many veterans use the system quite a bit and a small percent exploit it. So the attitude of the VA was well, "Jesus, he [the POW] couldn't have had much of a problem or he would have come to us 40 years ago." They simply cannot believe that it was predictable. And certainly, there was a norm for prisoners of war to not come for help.

Because if they talked about their problems, they would relive them, and that just triggers off more anxiety than they can possibly handle. So they just continued something that worked while they were prisoners of war—they shut out feelings that they couldn't handle. Most are still doing that.

Myself, I once in a while think, "Jesus, I remember how terrified I was when I was in combat." But I am just remembering it, I am not experiencing it. If you really start talking about those kinds of things, the emotions that are still there come out. You realize that at that time you are just hanging onto life. You don't know what is going to happen. People are doing all these inhuman things to you. How do you ever come to terms with it? It is just like a rape victim. They never really come to terms with the impact of that helpless experience unless they go to very carefully constructed counseling. It is just a totally overwhelming experience, and our society, until recently, never faced the fact that you would have these residuals. Now it is just well known. I think that is a tremendous gain. With the POW, you not only have the trauma, but you have the starvation and the brutality that depletes one's coping ability and one's body's ability, which eventually affects all aspects of one's system, even their immune systems and their abilities to cope with disease. All the professionals that have been involved in this agree that this is true.

As far as my POW experience and my time in the service is concerned, I was going to college and I joined the enlisted reserve, which was a program the Army put you on to get you to enlist but also to get you to finish college before going to active duty. They called all of us to active duty in the spring of 1943. I was then an infantry trainee at Camp Walters, Texas, and while I was in training, I broke my glasses. I'd only gotten in the infantry by convincing some guy to overlook the fact that I'd flunked my eye examination. Well, anyway, on the day we had to fire the Browning automatic rifle, I couldn't see without my glasses and shot up the target range, badly. I didn't hurt anybody, but they removed me from the infantry.

I then went before some review board where they try to find out what to do with you. I told them that I had enlisted in the Army and that I wanted to stay and do my part for the country, and I would do anything but be a medic. So they immediately put me in the medics! I was first a lab technician. Then after doing that a while, they sent me to Denver to be formally trained. I was just completing my training in Denver when I was called into the ASTP program [Army Specialized Training Program], and sent first to University of Nebraska for my preliminary assignment. Then I was later sent to Vanderbilt in Nashville, Tennessee. This was in the fall of '43. In early '44, they decided to close the program down which I was in. Then all of us in the program were assigned to various things. I was assigned to the medical detachment to the 425 Regional, 106th Division, and I was assigned to Company C as a combat medic. We went overseas to England in the fall of 1944. We trained a bit in England, then we were sent across the channel, in leaky boats, and landed in mid-November of 1944.

We then wound our way in trains and trucks to the front lines. We went through Luxembourg, and into the Siegfried line in Germany. The 106th Division was assigned to this area. We replaced the 2nd Division, which was a fighting division. Incidentally, our division was so ill-trained even before we got into combat, I felt no danger because I never thought we would ever have a combat assignment of importance. But oddly enough, we were the farthest outfit into Germany at the time. We were located exactly where the Battle of the Bulge started. We heard the German tanks way off in the distance warming up, but still no one thought too much of it. They were shelling us, too, but it seemed erratic, just enough to keep people honest. Then December 16, we were informed that we were surrounded. We had been in no particular battles at that particular time, but everyone was getting nervous. It was also real foggy and there was a good chance that if we started firing, we'd probably hit each other. Nervous troops tend to accidentally do that. I was a little busy taking care of some wounded but no one was hurt too badly, except one man that went berserk when the Germans surrounded our position. One guy was so on guard that when he pulled out the pin of one of his hand grenades, they thought he was a German spy. He ran, but they shot and killed him. Things were very confusing at that time.

At any rate, on December 18, our group was ordered to break out, to attack to the rear. It was cold as hell and we had to cross a roaring stream, waded across the thing, at dusk. So we got up the other side and the Germans are waiting for us and they hammered the hell out of us. Everyone was killed or wounded, at least almost everyone. Incidentally, here I was, a brand new medic and in combat. I had never been trained how to handle wounded under winter conditions, let alone in the dark.

We were being hammered. Mortars are firing all over the place. I am hiding under my helmet, so to speak, when I heard some guy start to scream, "Medic!" My first reaction was, "You son of a bitch. Now I have to get up." I was scared to death. But I got up and did what I could do, all I could do. The wounded are often confused as hell. They don't even know where they are wounded. One guy was telling me that it was either his foot or his leg, and here I am trying to cut his pants off to find out where he is wounded. Later I found out that he had been hit in the head, the eye to be exact. It all happened so quickly. One minute the German mortars are roaring and the next minute the battlefield is quiet except for the wounded. Another thing that we learned rather rapidly was that your morphine freezes in cold weather. You tried to give somebody a shot to reduce their pain but you couldn't get the morphine in them.

When night came on, it was cold as hell. We hadn't had much food on the front lines for several days. We had these wounded there, and some of them were dying. I remember this one guy that was shot through his stomach died, and I knew he was going to, but you learn fast in those conditions. At any rate, as morning was coming another medic and I put a bandage, the only thing we had white, on a stick and we walked across the battlefield waving the thing, hoping we weren't going to get shot. We wanted to get some help from the Germans because we knew they were the only ones around. They responded very well. A German officer saw us and ordered his soldiers to help us. We had about fourteen wounded guys, and the other medic and myself carried them all into a German Aid Station. Anyhow, the Germans were helpful to us on the front lines. I was really amazed that they were, thank God. When we carried the last ones over, I said to the German officer "Well, thank you. I am going to go back now."

It was just a bluff. I don't know what I meant by it. I wouldn't know where to go.

He said, "You can't do that."

I said, "I am a combat medic and we are under the Geneva Convention. We are not combative."

So he said, very cleverly, "Why don't you stay and take care of your comrades?"

Well, I had no choice anyhow. I took care of as many of our wounded that came in as I could. The Germans were too busy with other things to help out much in that regard. There was one guy, a medic, who was shot through the knee who was real bad, who was put on an ambulance and taken away. The rest of us just sat there.

Then the Germans marched us. They marched us 60 kilometers straight. Whether you were wounded or not, you marched. The other medics and I were taking care of those we could. It was bitter cold. We marched over what seemed like a mountain. We marched for a whole day. Then they put us in kind of a walled compound for the second night and told us that if anyone moved they would machine gun us all. We realized that they meant it, too.

Then they took us to a railroad station and they put us on boxcars with no medical attention, no food. Everyone is really in a weakened and starving condition. We are in the boxcars and at the time the fog that had caused the first part of the battle to go in Germany's favor lifted. Now anything that moves is being shot at by American airplanes. Here we are in the boxcars and on Christmas Eve. We are in the switchyard and right in the switchyard we get bombed. The cars start falling off the tracks. We all seemed to break out of the cars by the same time, because the German guards were hiding from the bombs. I then began to take care of people who were wounded from the bombing. I got to one guy who had his leg blown off. I did what I could to put a tourniquet around it. We then carried this guy and the other wounded men. When we got to our destination, someone else took him over. I have no idea what happened to the man.

It is Christmas Day and all the Germans could muster to give us to eat was a little grass soup and a tiny piece of bread. We were sleeping in tents by that time, and we were frozen and miserable. Because I was a medic, I was assigned to one of the buildings that had been hit by a direct blast of a bomb. The building housed 70 American physicians. I was given the terrible job of going around and getting bits of identification on these guys. I don't really remember too much more about it. You really are in a numb state. Nothing hits you very hard. I am a psychologist by training, and as you may know, people protect themselves by going into a state of shock. You just do things without any feeling at all. We were there for a very short period of time. Then they put us back in boxcars, and we headed across Germany in the direction of Berlin. Locked in these boxcars with no food, no water, and freezing; frostbite was everywhere. It was really miserable conditions, and the Germans provided absolutely nothing.

Once you get to the front lines, they were very tough and indifferent to you. It is understandable. Their country is being blown apart on a regular schedule. Life becomes very cheap.

Then we ended up at another camp. At Luckenwald, as stated under the Geneva Convention, officers, including non-commissioned officers, are separated from privates so they don't have to work.

Then we were taken into Berlin. There is a suburb of Berlin called Wuensdorf. It is where the German high command was located. We were in a very small stockade. I became the main medic for the prisoners in our camp, and ours was a work camp. Guys were falling over left and right from shoveling coal, their wounds, whatever.

We didn't have much in the way of equipment. But, surprisingly, none of the guys died from their wounds. I think they were young, and they had been inoculated. But you really don't recover. I had a cut on my hand. Because you don't get any food you are starving, and even a little cut doesn't heal. We didn't get anything to eat, at any rate. We were in this camp and we were bombed frequently. Our camp was bombed directly a few times. So we had wounded. I became kind of a doctor. I even did some minor surgery, really minor. Like I would have a leg all swollen up with infection and I would just have to cut it and drain the pus out of it.

Every morning, there was sick call. The Germans would make us all go out. Everyone was sick, but you just had to pick up the ones that were the sickest. One poor guy had rheumatoid arthritis and he couldn't move a muscle in his body, flat on his back. The only way he could move at all was if you moved things for him.

Since I was a medic, I didn't have to do any hard labor but I would go along with the guys, saying that I had to take care of them in case of a bomb raid. The whole point in the German camp was to try and bribe Germans. We would bring them cigarettes and then we would steal a little food. One day we were there and I am with the group and a bombing raid starts. The bombing was right on us. Well, the bombs start to fall and everybody runs. The Germans don't care too much about you during a time like that. Another American and I, this guy from Georgia, he and I ran into this building, a big army building, and then into the basement of it. It turned out to be the German's headquarters for defending the city. They didn't care that we were there. But this guy I was with had stolen some champagne and he was drunk. Then he starts singing, "I am rambling wreck from Georgia Tech." It was unbelievable. The Germans were all around us. It was incredible, unrealistic that something like that could happen.

As time moved on, we starved. So we got real good at taking advantage of the regular bombings to steal food. The only hitch was that we had to sneak it back into camp. But I became real good at that. What we did was we tied the sleeves of our coats and I put whatever goods or champagne I stole down each sleeve. Then when the Germans frisked us, all we had to do was remove our coats so they wouldn't find our goods. We managed to steal quite a bit of food, including some of the guys even stole some German medals, like the Iron Cross. When the Germans found that out, they were very angry at us. Things were very unpredictable at that time. Word had gone out that Hitler had ordered all the prisoners killed. We were very nervous, but we knew that the Allies were not far away. The Russians were coming in from the East and we started to see the new German jets flying overhead. They were really incredible.

They took us out of this camp and they marched us toward the west. Our guards were old men, and some of the prisoners were even carrying the guards' guns for them. We marched for three or four days to a huge prison camp. In that camp were Russians and 50,000 people. I meant to tell you earlier that in our work camp, everyone got jaundice and hepatitis, including myself. I started getting it the day we began our march. Hepatitis is a liver condition that can kill you. You turn a yellowish orange. Near the end I was very sick.

Around that time, a couple of British soldiers parachuted into our camp on purpose and permitted themselves to be captured. They were there to see our camp commandant. They met with the commandant and told him to surrender the camp to them. For if he didn't do that, he would be tried as a war criminal. The commandant turned the camp over to them. He then gathered thousands of prisoners around him, stood on a box, and made a speech that was interpreted in about six different languages, explaining what a good person he had been. And he begged the prisoners to stay inside the walls of the camp. The Russians who were there were really crazy, though. They kept breaking out of the camp and getting shot. Then one day, a truce was arranged on the front lines and the Red Cross was brought through. They took us wounded and sick out of there. We crossed the front lines on May 3. We were the rattiest people they'd ever seen. I don't even think that I washed my hands even once the whole time I was a prisoner. I had blood on them. We were covered with lice.

Of course, the first thing they did was delouse us. Then, on May 7th, we were sent to France and then on to Camp Lucky Strike. But we were never given any physical examinations or anything like that. No one thought to ask for one or complain about not getting one. You just lined up for food and were so damn delighted to be back. From that time on, sick or not, you never complained. You ate whatever food you could get, and they were feeding us very well by that time.

In June, we were put on ships to be sent home. Everyone was still worried about submarines, because half of the German Navy wouldn't know that they had surrendered, or they would think, "To hell with it." We landed in Boston, and the first thing I did was to go see an optometrist I had left a pair of glasses with before the war. Amazingly, he still had them.

From then on, we were treated pretty well. I ended up, for a while, in Miami Beach, in one of the R and R camps. I was even given a physical examination. I had had frozen feet and hepatitis. I was also still suffering from diarrhea. I got out of the military on December 24, 1945, and tried to get home for Christmas.

In my case, while I was a prisoner in this camp, I spent the majority of my time helping other POWs deal with their illness, helping them realize what they were going to get and what they weren't going to get. Much of my work was psychological, which made me much more aware of the need for this. For example, one guy wanted to insist that he was ill and that he had a bad back, so I said that if it didn't clear by the next day that I would have to do surgery. I thought that might traumatize him, and, of course, it did. His back recovered enough so he could get by. I just tried to give guys the hope they need to go on. Most were just lost in a stunned, depressed state. Most even stopped writing home, even though the Germans gave us stationery and everything.

Mario Garbin

Although Mario Garbin's internment was relatively short (five months), it was extremely severe nonetheless. For by the date of his capture, the Germans were running out of food, ideas, and patience, and the POWs became more of a nuisance than ever. In an effort to protect the POWs, then use them for barter, the POWs were at times marched, often without food, from dawn to dusk. During his imprisonment, Mario dropped from 195 pounds to 129, and he was considered one of the luckier ones. His story picks up a few days after his company had been overrun by the Germans.

Mario was one of the more fortunate POWs who put to use in his later life what he learned from his incarceration. At present, he is retired from over twenty years' service with the Chrysler Corporation, where he was a high-ranking vice president within the company, reporting directly only to the chairman of the board. Although powerful and charismatic, he still cried uncontrollably during one portion of the interview and had to pause several times to keep his composure in other portions. A copy of a story written by Mario, titled, "Christmas Story," which he feels most appropriately depicts his frame of mind during this time, is included in Appendix C.

A battalion motor pool had blocked the roadway up the hill with their trucks to prevent German tanks and armed vehicles from moving in to attack our troops. Sure enough, we went in there and here these guys came up to us and said, "What the hell is happening?" They'd been there two or three days. The Germans had just gone around them, leaving them in one of those little pockets they were so famous for. It was Blitzkrieg.

Speed in, isolate units, and keep racing forward. Their main destination reached, they would return to clean up later.

After we told them all that we knew, they suggested that we dig in along with everybody else. So we dug into the frozen ground, cut down trees and made foxholes that held two or three guys and built four layers of logs over it because we thought that they'd be firing tree bursts, shells that exploded above ground height and rained down into our foxholes. So for night after night, we'd just sit or stand there with weapons at the ready, wondering what the hell was going on and when the hell the Germans would be back to get us. We'd just sit there and watch those B-1s, the buzzbombs, come frequently over us on their way to England. We'd fire at them hoping to hit one.

One night a voice blared out of the darkness. It was the Germans. They had set up a series of loudspeakers. "Hey, fellows," they said in American English, "what the hell you wanna stay up there and freeze your ass off for? Hell, you're up to your ass in water."

And they were right. With all the snow that was melting from inside those logs that we used to cover our foxholes, we were sometimes ankle deep in ice water. It was cold, just so cold.

Then they keep going by saying things such as "Hey, fellas, why don't you come on over? We've got hot food, hot dogs, and good stuff. Come on in for a hot shower and clean sheets," which really broke us up. Shit, we hadn't seen sheets since we left the U.S., and we sure as hell knew they didn't have any. They played popular American songs which we really appreciated but sure as hell didn't lure anyone.

This went on for days. We spent them on perimeter guard duty night and day, felled more trees for protection, and watched our rations getting smaller and smaller. The rations were from the motor pool guys we joined on the hill. There was constant tree burst artillery shells coming on.

One day, while I was on perimeter duty, I saw a white flag being waved from the woods about 100 yards downhill. I was part of the regimental combat intelligence squad under the command of Lieutenant Thomas, the G2 or intelligence officer. I immediately went to him and together we went to Major Moon, the executive officer who took over the regiment when our battalion commander was fatally wounded. He'd been killed by a log blown out of the roof of our dug-in headquarters in an artillery barrage two days after the beginning of the Battle of the Bulge. My intelligence squad was also quartered there. With Lieutenant Thomas, I went forward to meet the white flag after we yelled that we'd meet halfway.

Out of the woods had walked a SS sergeant, black uniform, (*Tottenkopf*) death's head insignia, highly polished boots and all. He was the epitome of military courtesy, saluting, and so forth. After introducing himself in perfect English, he began his pitch.

"I'm authorized to guarantee you protection under the Geneva Convention if you surrender now. If you decide not to surrender now, that's okay too. But I want you to know that we've advanced at least ten miles past your position already, and when we have time we're going to come back and clean you up. Then we won't ask you to surrender. We'll just get rid of you. We won't want to be bothered. Fellows," he says, "let me tell you something. I was a prisoner twice of you Americans and you guys really treated me right. I appreciated that. This isn't a trick. If you don't agree to come out, you're dead. Think hard and take good advice. Come out honorably."

We took him to Major Moon and the battalion officer staff.

Well, even though we at first thought that this guy's speech was just another one of their psychological ploys, he must have made one hell of an impression on our commanding officer. For after conferring with regimental staff, Moon agreed to a surrender under certain conditions. We were given 36 hours to ready ourselves for an honorable surrender. Nobody seemed to be too stunned by the whole scenario except this one guy who had come to us after fleeing from Poland and joining the U.S. Army. He had lost his mother and sisters to atrocities. He was raging. He couldn't believe we were going to surrender. He just went crazy. He tried to kill Moon. Finally, we had to knock him to the ground and tie him up.

On the morning of our surrender, some of the guys started rigging their weapons to explode in the face of any German who cared to fire them. Some took out parts of the trigger assembly and buried them. They also poured dirt and all the sugar we had into the gas tanks of our vehicles.

When we marched out, they were waiting for us. We didn't know what they were going to do, but they treated us well. They let us come out with our weapons and thrown them on a pile. Then they lined us all up and we marched, and marched, and marched for a few days, until we finally got to these trains they had for us. We hadn't eaten a bit of food since we'd surrendered. So they gave us each one big hunk of bread with a gob of molasses on it. I started to find out, firsthand, just how irrational people can be. This guy in front of me, a Southerner, turned around to me and started bitching. "This goddamn stuff is molasses," he said, pointing to the goo on top of the bread.

"I know," I replied.

"Well, I don't eat this shit," he said as he handed it to me.

I tried to hand it back to him saying, "We don't know when we're going to get to eat again."

"I don't eat molasses," he said again, turning away. "That stuff is for the pigs."

I tried to convince him no more and gladly ate the gift he had given me.

Shortly after, they began stuffing us in boxcars, at least 70 to a car. We were packed in there so tight that there was barely room to sit, let alone lie down. If we had to move, we did so in concert with each other. There was only one little window in the corner of that thing too. What came through that was about all the light we got. There were separated planks in the walls which also let in some light and frigid air. If you had to go, you went right where you sat. Some guys used their steels [helmets].

We were a sorry sight, and it didn't take long before guys started getting sick. Some had trenchfoot. Others began to get fevers. On only our second night in these cars, a guy not too far away from me began to die. He was just burning up from a fever, was real flushed and began crying out for water. So we gave him some, but we ran out quickly, or at least we thought we did. Then some son of a bitch, an American, a few places down said, "I'll give you a drink for five bucks. I got a full canteen." I forgot who said it, but somebody told him the equivalent of where that canteen was going to end up lodged if he didn't hand it over. He handed it over all right, but he bitched about it the entire way.

"Goddamn, I was saving that for myself," he said.

I just couldn't believe what I had heard. It was the beginning of an experience that changed my whole life. I saw so much of it but I never got used to it. It's amazing how quickly people give up that American idealism of sharing, caring and working together and quickly switch to an "I/me" philosophy when the going gets tough. I just couldn't stomach it and refused to acknowledge such actions. But they hurt me, affected me deeply, nonetheless.

But early the next morning, they were back. "Raus, raus mit uns! Raus mit uns! [Out]" And they marched us for several days, parking us anywhere they could, barns, open fields, whatever, every night. Finally, they got us to an RR marshalling spot and took us to our first POW camp. It was near Munich. I thought it was 4B.

The first thing they did at that camp was delouse us. They made us drop all our clothes and parade into a large shower stall. At first, we wondered if we'd be getting showered or gassed, because we'd already begun to hear what Hitler was doing to the Poles and Jews and others. A little English soldier who was passing out small bars of soap saw that I was a little hesitant about turning on my shower, so he came over to me and said, "Don't worry, you're really going to take a shower."

I couldn't believe it, I was really taking a shower. As I let the water just run down over me, this Brit asked me, "What's your rank, Yank?"

"I'm a private first class," I replied.

"Make yourself a non-com," he whispered.

"What?" I asked, somewhat startled.

"If you're a private," he said, "they make you work under the Geneva Convention protection. If you're a non-com, they can't make you work. You gotta pen?"

I nodded that I did. That day I promoted myself to a staff sergeant by changing the classification in my paybook, which was the last thing most

GIs would throw away. So it was always a safe bet for the Germans that they could check our paybooks for verification of our rank.

After that I was assigned to a barracks. Mine happened to be filled with a lot of Brits.

The Brits were very organized. Some of them had been there for over four years. They were survivors. A lot of them had been taken at Dunkirk or had been captured by Rommel in North Africa. But there was a significant difference between they and us. They were seasoned. They were disciplined, and they got to resent the GIs' easy and loose discipline. They began to look upon us as second-class citizens. But they knew what they were doing and did it well.

Even though supplies were extremely scarce and in short supply, they still had tea every day. They made it with sugar and powdered milk from these care packages we received. They were always clean shaven and such. And each one seemed to have their own idiosyncrasies. One guy played the bagpipes. He used to drive us nuts. But then he used to drive nuts even the other Scots. Some did Shakespearean readings to entertain their colleagues. Others did lectures. One guy used to be the chief guard at Dartmoor Prison in England. He gave a lecture on the English prison system. I just used to say to myself, "I don't believe this." They were so organized. It was great. They were very military, as were the Germans. By God, when they saw an English officer it was salute, attention, relax. They treated you like a soldier. If you didn't act like a soldier, you got belted. They used to scream at us, "Don't you Americans have any pride?" Because our guys used to just slouch around and say back to the Brits, "I'm not going to salute that fucking son of a bitch." Some of us tried to pull our guys aside and talk some logic to them. I mean, these Brits had been here for four years. We could learn something from them. Most of us wised up eventually. Well, at least, those of us who survived did.

At this camp, we were allowed to write a postcard home and to keep half a blanket. We stayed there only until the middle of January or so, when we were packed into another train and sent east to a camp near the Czech border. We stayed until Ash Wednesday before we were moved again.

This camp was made up pretty much of a real collection, Serbs, Belgians, Frenchmen, Brits, us, New Zealanders, you name it. In a certain part of the camp, isolated completely from us, were the Italians and Russians. The Russians had been isolated because the Germans believed them to be animals and because they didn't subscribe to the Red Cross; the Italians because they were viewed as traitors, since they had switched sides from the Germans to the Americans when they surrendered.

I've always had a certain facility for language. I had picked up enough German to be able to maneuver with the guards, and I spoke fluent Italian, which enabled me to do a lot of trading. There was this Greek guy in our camp who had taught me the ropes. He used to get out of camp every day, and I asked him how he did it. "Two cigarettes to the guards at a certain time of the day and they'll let you get into the Russian camp where the Italians also were."

Well, I knew that if I got to where the Italians were that I could really communicate. What made these guys so special was that they used to get out each day to go work in the surrounding towns. We, as non-coms, couldn't. These guys used to take out your jewelry, fountain pens and such and bring back bread and things of that sort. Cigarettes became the money of trade. I used to smoke a pack a day before I became a prisoner. But I cut back to almost nothing because I needed them to trade. Though sometimes I would get away with trading half a cigarette or so for some guy's daily ration of bread. Then I'd save the other half to smoke myself.

So upon the advice of this Greek guy, I went to the fence at the time he told me would be best and handed the guard two cigarettes and he let me through. I later found out that I could get through by just cutting a small hole in the fence. That way I could save some of my cigarettes. But anyway, I got into the Russian camp and oh, how they gathered around me there. The Italians were the first to approach me.

"You're American?"

"Yes," I'd reply.

"Ahhh."

They wanted to know what the hell had been happening with the war, and I told them. I struck some bargains. I'd bring stuff in and they would bring me back whatever. So I became a trader. I fed a small group of guys who were with me for a few months by doing that. And the Russians used to come up also. They'd go through the latrine window and do their trading. We'd give them our sweaters and they'd give us bread. As you can imagine, I lost a great deal of weight, but I managed to survive longer than most guys just through my trading. But it's amazing what hunger will do to a person. They lose all perspective, all respect for themselves.

There is one episode seared in my mind that shows what hunger, and perhaps lack of desire, can do to even allegedly disciplined men. Thank God it represents a very small percentage of GIs.

One day the Serbian POWs in our compound, all of whom worked in near-by factories, etc., sent a representative to the American barracks to talk to us. An American of Serbian ancestry translated. The gist of the talk: "We respect and admire America. You Americans have much less food [rations] than we have. We will donate one day's ration to you tomorrow." An amazingly generous offer in a place where food was more precious than diamonds. Sure enough, several strapping Serbians carried in large wooden tubs of rice with little bits of meat in them. We lined up with our tin cans to get a share. I was sitting on a top bunk eating my rice with a guy I hadn't met before. In a few minutes our Serb translator said, "There's some left. They want you to line up and they'll dish it out until the tubs are empty."

Many of our guys yelled and charged the tubs, overturned them, and scraped rice off the floor (which was covered with dirt and dried diarrhetic shit) like crazed animals. The guy next to me had not yet eaten his rice. He looked at that scene, looked at me, jumped off the bunk, and walked over to a cluster of guys fighting for the rice on the floor. He turned his filled tin can over, spilling his rice on the heads and backs and asses of those guys, and with a tone of unbelievable disgust and revulsion yelled, "Here's some more pigs. Show those guards what lousy animals Americans are." He left. I never saw him again.

I even began to catch a little hell, because I wasn't doing that bad, with my trading and everything. In fact, one day a staff sergeant who knew me in regimental headquarters came up to me and threatened to tell the Germans that I was only a private. He was just jealous because I was doing all right. I just couldn't believe the gall of the guy. Putting me down for showing a little initiative.

I told him, "Get off your ass and go out and do something yourself," I said. "How the hell do you think I'm getting through?" Most of our guys just sat around all day and talked about home, their mother's cooking and exchanging recipes. They could have tried to trade.

But the guy didn't give a shit. He threatened to tell anyway. So I found a little ploy that worked almost every time. I was in charge of cutting, for my squad, the loaf of bread the Germans used to give us every day. That was a real big deal. So I was allowed a knife about three or four inches long. I took the knife and went up to this weakass sergeant and held it up to his throat and I said, "The day you say something about my rank to the Germans is the day that this knife will be going into your throat." The son of a bitch just turned as yellow as one can get. Some of the other guys in our group began yelling for me to kill him. I never even had to approach the guy about the subject again. But it was just indicative of the lengths some guys will go when they're hungry, and I was doing my best to use whatever abilities I had to help feed ourselves. But yet he became envious of me. For some reason, nobody knew I was bluffing about killing a fellow GI.

Guys just became thieves. You know, the one small loaf of bread was all we were rationed as a group of eight every day. But once in a great while we'd get a little something extra, like a can of tuna. We'd take turns getting the can after the tuna was split. At first they began to come in relatively often. Then these little extra packages would begin to come in once every two weeks. You can't image what hunger is until you go through this type of thing, to watch a guy simply rubbing his finger over and over again inside an empty can and licking it, over and over again just to get a little taste of the tuna.

I used to eat part of my tuna ration and then save some for a later day. Well, this one day, I had this tuna. I made a little tuna sandwich. Most of us had a little box that held our meager possessions. That's where you kept all your treasures. I had this sandwich in there wrapped in some paper and I used to sleep with my hand on this little box. Son of a bitch, one morning when I woke up somebody had gotten into the box and stolen my little sandwich. If I'd caught the guy, I would have killed him. But our guys just had no compunction. Their attitude was, "I'm gonna survive. If you don't, tough shit." The stealing got worse as time went on.

The British handled their guys differently. When they caught a thief, they really took care of them. One day they caught this guy and made an announcement to the entire camp that he was a thief. Then they took and threw him into a latrine, which was no more than just a big bowl dug out of the ground full of diarrhetic slop.

The Russians, those poor guys. They used to have to empty the latrines. They had a honey wagon, a big barrel pulled by two horses, and they had a big hose attached to some sort of big suction thing. They'd put the hose in the latrine to pump it out and shit from the latrines would just start squirting all over them. Those poor Russians. The Germans just treated them like animals.

Sickness, weakness, and starvation began to accelerate. It even got to the point where you got to know when a guy was going to die. In the morning you'd wake up and look at the fellas around to see whose face was swollen, beginning to swell from edema, I guess. His heart was beginning to fail. And in a day or two, inevitably, this guy would be dead. So you'd wake up in the morning and there'd be one or more guys in there who'd died during the night. We'd tell the Germans. They'd bring in a box or boxes, whatever we needed for burial. The Germans would also give us an American flag to put on the coffin. At first this really bothered me, to have one of our own guys die. But then it became so routine that you just didn't feel anymore. You'd put the guy in his box, carry him out, bury him and that was it. No feelings at all. You just did what you had to do. Some GIs started to refuse to even help carry the guy out to be buried. They just didn't care. They'd just say, "Fuck 'em, he's dead." It got to the point where we couldn't even get four guys together to carry a box out. The Germans, who are very disciplined, just couldn't understand. They couldn't fathom how we could be so uncaring about our dead buddies. They just couldn't comprehend our lack of respect. As a result, they began getting irritated with us. They occasionally threatened some of our guys and making them do it.

There were a lot of deaths. Some caught scarlet fever. Some got trenchfoot. They had to bandage them up with whatever they could since we didn't have any bandages. Usually, they used tissue paper or something. We also had no medicine. So inevitably any guy that caught something serious usually died. As we found out after the war, TB was not uncommon.

I used to just dread every morning for the thought that I would wake up with diarrhea. For if you got that, it means that you had dysentery. If it continued, you were a goner. These places had no heat, by the way, and they gave you only half a blanket. And I used to have a recurrent dream that my mother would come to me in the barracks at night with a suitcase full of Clark Bars, which I loved. She'd say, "Eat, Mario." I would devour them, but never get filled. When I awoke, one side of my field packet would be streaked with saliva. She used to always send them to me when I was at college. I just couldn't get enough. My mother used to use a lemon face cream at night. In my dreams I could actually smell the lemon. You had to remain hopelessly optimistic to survive, dream that you would someday be breathing in your mother's lemon face cream again. Some guys just totally focused on the end of the war. They started saying that they felt, or just knew that the war was going to be over in 90 days. It gave them something to live for. Pretty soon other guys began to believe. Soon they began wagering on the exact date that the war would end. It kept them alive, gave them a reason to live.

And sure enough, we got the order one day that we were going to be moved out. The Russians were advancing fast into our region from the East, and they were going to use us as bargaining tools. So we began to take on a little value to them. So they told us on this Tuesday, the one before Ash Wednesday, that we'd be moving out. We started out walking that next morning. We walked every day from Ash Wednesday to Good Friday. First, we went west. And then north, and then back down south, and then east, and then west and then back up north. Each morning they would come in and wake us at dawn. Usually, we slept in barns or bombed out factories, and we walked until it was dark. By that time, things were getting really bad. Many of the guys had taken ill. We all had those big, fat, gray lice and fleas. We began taking off our socks to wear over our hands just to keep them warm.

Amazing, I had this watch. [He points to the watch on his wrist.] My mother gave it to me in 1939. The band expands on it. When we were first captured, they told us to put our arms out straight in front of us. Then when they saw a watch or a ring or something, they'd pull it off. But I slid the watch to up around my upper arm so that they couldn't see it. So they didn't see it. I just can't imagine that I was able to bring it back with me. It's been through so much. I wear it to this day.

Well anyway, on these marches, some days you got soup, bread. It all depended upon whether the food wagons showed up that day or not. Guys started to go even more crazy on these marches. I don't know how many miles we went, but we had about 1,600 guys when we started out. Near the end of the march, we didn't have 500. They were falling like flies.

Who knows what happened to them or what the Germans did with them. They just disappeared, but they fell like flies.

They always marched us up along the back roads, never along the Autobahn. And we always passed these fields where there were these huge earthen mounds, where sugar beets, potatoes and such were stored. There were always guards around us, too, with dogs trained to attack. We'd stop every two hours for a ten-minute rest, and you were told not to leave the side of the road. If you did, you would be shot or the dogs would be sent after you. We always had the Douglas Fairbanks in the crowd. The first stop, a couple of guys said they were going to take off. We told them they were crazy. We were near the Czech border, and they couldn't even speak German. I don't know if they were beginning to get delusional or what, but sure enough these guys roll into some nearby bushes. The dogs, hearing the bushes move, went instantly on alert. And one of the dogs just ahead of me was just dying to get off his leash. The guards had a very nice way of showing you what they mean, and they didn't do it slowly. So you get the picture real quick. So the guard in front of me unsnapped his dog's leash, and he went after one of the guys and killed him. The guard and his buddies, who had also released their dogs as well, took their good old sweet time getting to the woods. There were four guys originally who had tried to escape. Only two came out of the woods. The dogs had torn the throats of the other two. They didn't even come out of the bushes. So one guard turned to us and said, "You guys get the picture?"

What the dogs had done to their buddies didn't seem to matter to some guys, because they'd just take off when they saw one of those mounds. The guards would just nonchalantly send the dogs after them. Do you think it would stop them? No way. The Germans then began shooting some of the guys. This one guard just strolled up to two guys that have dug into the mounds and are eating sugarbeets or whatever. He pulled out his pistol and—tump, tump—and shot both in the head. The guys were just out of control. Even that display didn't stop some guys from trying later on. That guard played that scenario on other occasions. The guards, by the way, were mostly non-Germans from countries conquered by the Nazis and were willing to side with them. Some were sadistic.

In all reality though, we were pretty lucky. We had this captain who was in charge. He was a man of good will. He protected us. He had two sons in American prisoner of war camps. After all this marching, we ended up near Brounsweig, about 30 miles west of Berlin. The last few weeks though, more and more of us started getting real dizzy and close to blacking out. So anyway, I felt the right time had come to try something. So I said to myself, 'Are you going to die like these poor bastards, or are you going to try and do something about it?' For two or three days we had been hearing what we thought was thunder. One guy who had been in the artillery said, "Thunder, hell. Those are our guys. Those are our

105 howitzers." Then a few of us began thinking about it. If we got away, maybe we could just hide out in the woods and steal from the farms and whatever until our forces arrived.

I got five of our guys together one night after we housed in barns to sleep. I said, "I'm not going to die by a roadside. I want to take off. You interested?" They said yes. We worked out a plan.

All marching columns had a horse-drawn "crank wagon" [sick wagon] at the tail end to pick up guys who couldn't absolutely walk, and every column had a half-dozen or more guard dogs with their handlers. For the past few days, I'd noticed there were no dogs with handlers, and for two days there was no sick wagon. In the hope that the dogs and wagon wouldn't be present tomorrow, I suggested we take off in the early part of tomorrow's march. I was to drop off first and if the other five guys saw I made it, they'd drop off every 30 or 40 yards also. I dropped off to the side of the road, dropped my trousers to my ankles. My legs looked like sticks. All of us had lice and flea bites that we'd scratch in our sleep and so our legs were covered with scabs. I picked off about a dozen scabs, smeared the pus and blood that was under the scabs and smeared the mess on my legs. I then sat there trying to look even more pathetic than I did. In a few minutes or so, the guard with the column came along, came up to me and said, "March."

I said, "I can't."

He cocked his rifle, pointed it at me and repeated his order. I decided to roll the dice. In German, the words for "shoot" and "shit" are "shiessen" and "scheissen". I couldn't remember which was which. I used one of them: "Scheissen" [shoot]. He hesitated, looked at me fixedly, at my sorry-looking legs and body, and a look of sympathy passed over his face. He whistled to the next guard to alert him I was there. The next guard also stopped. We went through the same routine, except I said, "I'll wait for the sick wagon." He said there wasn't one. I said, "Ja, ja" [yes, yes]. He also looked at me with pity, smiled and went on. They knew the end for them was near and I guess they were sick of the whole thing themselves. He went on. I just couldn't believe it! The column just passed me by. I started edging to the side of the road and I just lay there. Then I noticed a few guys coming my way. It was our small escape band. The scheme worked for them too.

We had all saved a little food. Some Belgian POWs had taught us what to do with our bread, to put it in a warm place so it would become hard-tack. We also had saved a few rations. We had enough to eat for a couple of days. So after just lying in the bushes for a while, we decided that we'd start checking around for a farm or something after it got dark. Hopefully, we'd find one, steal some food and then head back into the woods again. So we waited until the sun was just beginning to go down before heading out of the bushes. Then just as we did, a horse drawn wagon came by.

It was driven by a German soldier. He glanced over at us as we dove back into the bushes. So we just laid there, not moving at all. Then ten or 15 minutes later, he came back again. He didn't even look our way this time, so we stayed put. Then about an hour later, another wagon came by. Two men were at the seat of the wagon. One was a German officer. The wagon stopped approximately where we are lying. The other man spoke to us in English. "We know you are there. Come out and we will not harm you," he said.

He looked like a Tatar or someone from one of those little republics who had been pressed into service by the Germans. "I am a doctor," he continued, "I am not a Nazi. Come out and we will treat you according to the Geneva Convention."

We didn't know if we should believe this guy or if he was bullshitting us. But what the hell were we going to do? They knew we were there. So I decided to take the first chance, so I stood up. "Come, please," he says, "I am not a Nazi. I am a doctor." So he motioned for me to get into the wagon. The other guys followed. He took us back to this lazaret, a hospital. Damn, all the guys there seemed to be Russians dressed in German uniforms. They took us to some shower stalls and told us to get cleaned up, and they gave us these floppy grass slippers and striped PJs, the ones usually worn by political prisoners, to put on when we were done. Then we were taken into a room with beds, and they served us some food, bread, sausage. Though there was a lot of food, I couldn't resist hiding a little sausage for later. So I stuck some in my pocket. I just wanted to make sure that I'd have some for the next day. I did so without even realizing what I was doing, and I did some of that after it had just become way of life. Afterwards we went to sleep.

The next morning, one of these officers came in and began looking around. We tried to communicate with him. He spoke a little English. He took our names and serial numbers. Later he came back in and tried to give poor Bucky, a kid from Cincinnati, a shot. Poor Bucky, he'd lost so much weight that he looked like a corpse. He just started crying. He just ran to me. I guess that because I was older, 26, that he kinda looked at me like an older brother. "Please don't let them do it," he begged. He just didn't have any meat for them to get the needle into.

Basically, during our time there, we would eat and sleep, eat and sleep. And each time you woke up, you'd see somebody else new that they had brought in. So this one day I woke up and I nodded to them and said, "Glad you made it," and then rolled over to go back to sleep. Then it suddenly hit me. These guys were wearing steels, and they were armed. I snapped around and sat up and said, "You guys Americans?"

"Who the hell do we look like," one of them replied. "And who the hell are you?"

I said, "I'm a GI," and I showed them my dog tags. Just then Bucky, who's real excited, jumped out of bed, and they got a real good look at him.

The one guy said, "Holy shit! Who the hell did this to you guys?"

A couple of them flipped and they wanted to go out into the hospital and start shooting the personnel. I told them that the doctors weren't responsible for how we looked. You have no idea how these guys looked. I mean next to us they looked like John Waynes. Bucky even ran over and started feeling their biceps and saying, "Look at these all-Americans."

So anyway I asked these guys if they [the U.S. Army] were really that close. They replied that they themselves were lost, and that they had gotten so far ahead of their companies that they just figured they were in trouble. They were trying to get back to their lines. Then they told us to hold tight and that they'd send somebody to get us once they got back to their companies. But before leaving they emptied their pockets of all the candy bars and rations and gave them to us.

Sure enough, not a day or so later an American major showed up. But once he saw us, he jumped back about two feet and I had to explain to him that we were all Americans. For like the other guys, he didn't believe us at first either. When he left he promised to send an ambulance for us in a few days. Before he left he made it clear to our physicians that the way they would be treated by the Americans would depend on how we were treated by them.

In two days the ambulance did come, and they took us back behind the American lines. As we got out of the ambulance, there were GIs standing around watching us. They just kept asking each other, "Who in the hell are these guys?" Like the others, they too couldn't believe that we were Americans. Many of us, most particularly Bucky Walters from Cincinnati, looked like walking stick men.

Steve Perun

Steve Perun still lives with the nightmares of his incarceration, but he appreciates wholeheartedly the compassion of decent men and women whose paths he crossed. A hard-fighting realist, Steve broke into tears on four occasions during the following interview, each time in remembering an act of compassion either toward him or from him toward someone else.

We hit the third wave in the Normandy beachhead. I was in the 79th Infantry, the 314th Battalion, F Company. I was a machine gunner.

We hit the beachhead, and it was toward evening. When we hit, there was a lot of dead soldiers floating on top of the water, and we had to push them out of the way to make it to the shore. When we hit the shore, the Germans put down a barrage of artillery that was just terrifying. When the shells started to hit, I leaped into the nearest trench and landed on a dead German. I stayed there for quite some time, for all hell was breaking loose.

After that subsided, we moved on. The only way we could attack was from the rear because the Germans had these big guns facing the English Channel. But they couldn't fire them on us because we were attacking them from the rear.

The 79th and 36th Infantry took the area for General Patton to come into with tanks. Then we joined his Third Army. We had originally been with the Seventh. Our job with the Third Army was to follow Patton's tanks. But he was moving forward so fast with those tanks that we couldn't keep up with him. So we fell behind, and it wasn't too long before we found ourselves completely surrounded by Germans. We were trapped. So the 82nd Airborne was called in to rescue us. They dropped in about 1,500 troops with supplies. We were out of ammunition and everything. That was at St. Lô.

When the 82nd was being dropped in, one of their guys got shot up in the air and his leg was shattered, and he was just left laying in an open field. The Germans were starting to mount a counter-attack at the same time, with tanks, heavy artillery, and everything. So I ran over and pulled the guy out of the field and dragged him down into a ditch. If I would have left him out there he would have been a goner for sure, because those German tanks don't stop for nothing and they would have just run right over him. I didn't get his name or anything. I tried to locate him later to see if he made it, but I never could find him after that, and shortly after I dragged him to safety my company was forced to move out. So I never did know what happened to him.

In St. Lô, we lost many of our men in the hedgerows. It was hell, but we kept going on. Then, in about the fourth week after we had come ashore, I was on night patrol. By this time I had lost both of my assistant machine gunners. The first one had been killed by a hand grenade. I had been wounded about the same time as well. But I just kept firing. I bet I went through a half-million rounds. Patton was way, way ahead of us by that time. Like I said, we just weren't able to keep up. We'd been left behind to clean up the German pockets of resistance.

But back to this night patrol. It was on a Friday night, the 13th of the month when I was sent out. Our job was to infiltrate the German line and scout out their positions, which we did. But on our way out we ran right into a German machine gun. There were three of us. One of the other guys tried to get away and they killed him. Myself and the other guy, Lieutenant Price, were taken prisoner. They separated us shortly after, though, and I never saw Lieutenant Price after that.

Then the Germans took me into a civilian underground prison camp in Germany. They put me in a little 8-by-8 cell. I was locked inside with a civilian guy. I was so scared of him. He had gonorrhea. I was there for three days with him. In those three days, they stripped me down and took me to a German colonel to be interrogated. He wanted to know a lot of stuff and we, of course, weren't allowed to tell him anything. He slapped me around quite a bit. They took me to see this guy three times. Finally, on the third time he had gotten pretty fed up with me, and he asked me, "What are you fighting for?" [crying]

Anyway, I told him, "My country's at war."

He just looked at me and said, "You're a good soldier." Then he let me go.

By the time I returned to my cell after my final visit to the colonel, almost all of my clothes had been stolen, including my shoes, which were designed to keep our feet warm to 20°F. On my fourth day there, we were scheduled to move out. But I had no shoes. I had no socks. So the Germans gave me burlap sacks to wrap around my feet. Then they also gave me a pair of wooden shoes, which were supposed to keep me warm in the 14 or 15 inches of snow outside.

So we started marching, and I was lucky that I had a good guard. He was a wonderful fellow [crying]. Anyway, he'd stop and get us things to eat, a little hard bread, whatever, along the way. We marched for about a week and a half. We had to go to Stalag 7A in Munich. He did whatever he had to do along the way. He'd hitchhike a truck or whatever went by if he could. There were two of us POWs that he was guarding.

On the way, this guard hitchhiked this one truck, a supply truck. This guard gave me his gun to hold for him while he climbed into the truck. It was a real high truck. I could have shot everybody there and got away. But where in the world would I have gone?

So he got in the truck and I handed him his rifle. Then he pulled me up inside with him and I pulled the other guy up inside with us. Then we took a train later on, and another truck and on and on.

Further on down the line, our guard hitchhiked a car, and when we got inside there was this German colonel inside who asked me my name and everything. He then asked me what nationality I was. I told him that I was of English origin because I didn't want to tell him that I was Ukrainian. The Germans hate the Ukrainians. They hated the Poles, too. I figured that this colonel wouldn't know the difference. Then he asked me where my parents were from and I told him Liverpool, England. He believed me.

After that, we marched for another week or so, staying overnight in a lot of different places. This one night we stayed in a Gestapo office. Now they were mean. They were so mean. Ohhh. They were plain German. They put us in a cell and kept us there for two days, interrogating us regularly. They thought nothing of hauling off and hitting us in the face. They were mean, real mean.

Finally, we were put upon a cattle car. There was just me and this other guy, and all these poor-looking souls dressed in striped uniforms. We didn't know it at the time, but they were all Jews headed for death camps. We didn't know at the time what the Germans were doing to these poor people. That cattle car was quite a sight. There were frozen or half-frozen civilians laying all over. All they had to wear and keep them warm were these little, thin striped suits, and it was consistently −10°F. These cattle cars had no heat or anything to them and they were all opened up.

On the second day the Germans opened up the door and threw in a few loaves of hard bread. It was so hard that you could have pounded a nail with it. Well, as I'm sure you could imagine, everybody, all of whom were starving, just went wild over this stuff. But I tell you something, these people were sure cool under pressure. With everyone grabbing and calling for food, the guys that were in charge broke off just enough bread to pass around, ensuring that everyone got nearly the same amount. I thought that they were going to be killed for that food. But they knew how to handle the others. We were there in that boxcar for two or three days, and then the Germans took us out and we were on a march again.

Then we obviously must have been getting pretty close to our destination because we began to see POWs working along the railroad tracks. Somewhere along there, we ran into some American POWs digging for food, potato peels, anything, in a dump. So I talked to them and asked them why they were doing that.

The guy I asked that to just said, "Fella, you just wait. In a few weeks you'll be doing this too." And, by God, he was right.

In a few more days we got to Munich, where we were put to work, seven days a week, 12 hours a day. We worked hard. We used to get these Red Cross parcels, and they always had this good-smelling soap in them. So we'd cut the bars up into three different pieces. Then we'd trade the pieces for food with the civilians. They gave us anything that was eatable.

This one morning when we were getting ready to be shipped off on cattle cars over 30 miles to work, I decided to hide some of my Red Cross goodies under my pants and in between my legs. The Germans always asked us for anything that we were carrying before we left. They didn't want us to be doing any trading. But this one time I decided to sneak some stuff through. So when the Germans asked me for whatever I was carrying I told them that I didn't have anything. But there was this one big, one-eyed SS guard that didn't believe me. He just off and hit me, knocking me to the ground. He was going nuts on me. He was kicking me and everything. Another guard pulled him off me just in time because the one-eyed guy had pulled out his Luger and was going to finish me off.

When we were fed, we were lucky if we were given some watery rice soup, or some watery cabbage soup that had been made with the loose, outside leaves. When they gave us that soup, there'd always be a lot of cabbage worms floating around in it. They didn't even clean the cabbage before cooking it, obviously. When the worms were cooked, they turned real black. We got real good at picking them out of our soup. But we had to eat the soup. It was all we got.

When we were there, we used to get our news from the States through one guy in our barracks, who made a radio out of a crystal set he had come up with somehow. He'd even used a bladder from a cat that we killed for food for part of his earphone. During this time the Germans were handing us all kinds of propaganda. They said that New York had been bombed, Washington had been captured, all that. Well, anyway, this guy was giving us the news. The Germans found out somehow that we were getting news, so they came in our barracks and started searching all over.

Then they found this little tiny antenna wire and they traced the crystal set back to this guy. Then three big Germans came in and dragged the guy out of the barracks. There were three steps from the barracks to the ground. By the time he hit the third step he was dead. They had shot him through the head. We all saw it happen. Such things were not uncommon. We used to see guys getting shot all the time, especially on the way to work. The Germans would just shoot and kill them.

We were liberated on the 29th of April by the 14th Armored and the 99th Infantry. The 14th Armored were all colored soldiers. Well, I tell you, these colored soldiers were on tanks. I don't know if they were General Patton's men or not. So there was a big highway close to our camp and our planes hadn't been bombing it because it was too close to our camp. Three days before we were liberated, the Germans left us and our officers took over. They told us not to break camp.

We knew that the Americans were close, though, because we could see big flashes of light on the horizon and we could hear bombs going off in the distance and such. Then, in about a week and a half, our troops broke through the German resistance and came through our area. As they did, we all broke camp and flooded out onto the highway so even the troops couldn't pass without running over us.

The colored tank drivers started pleading with us to get out of the way because they had the Germans on the run and they were in hot pursuit. As close behind the Germans as they were, the Germans wouldn't have been able to blow up any bridges or anything in their retreat. So as fast as they could go, they had to go to keep close to the Germans.

These colored guys got out of their tanks [crying] and we began hugging them and kissing them. We were just so glad to see them because they were Americans. It was so nice to see them.

After we were liberated, we were supposed to be out of that camp within 48 hours. There was about 40,000 total of us POWs in the camp—Brits, Russians, Canadians, and a lot of others. But we ended up being there for over two weeks. Some English colonel was supposed to be in charge of getting us out. He was supposed to get us out within those 48 hours because after that time the Germans would have the ability to bomb our camp. We got lucky though, because they never did bomb.

But like I said, we held the 14th Armored tanks up. Then after we let them go, about 30 miles away they blew up a real big bridge and had a real big battle down there. Then they finally built a pontoon bridge across the river and were able to go back in hot pursuit of the Germans. But if we wouldn't have held them up, the Germans wouldn't have been able to blow up that bridge and slow our guys up. For, like I said, with the 14th so close behind them, the Germans wouldn't have had the time to blow up the bridge. All they had the time to do was run.

Since our guys were moving so fast through our position, and since that English colonel didn't move us out as fast as he was supposed to, we were forgotten. We didn't have any food or supplies or anything. We had to start combing the countryside and stealing and taking what we could. Finally, the 14th put up a kitchen and we started going there to eat. They were real buddies.

After that, General Patton appeared at the camp. In fact, he came into my barracks and he saw what condition we were in. We were all skin and bones, and bit up with lice and bed bugs. We had big sores on us and everything.

The next day, Patton had C-47 transport planes flying in from everywhere. They were landing in hayfields or anywhere they could put down. They were landing planes all over. So finally they got us out and took us to different hospitals in France, where I was for about a month and a half. My system was so out of whack that I had to start out on baby food.

This one time, back at camp, the Russians refused to go to work at night because they wouldn't be fed before going to work at night, and they wanted to be. So they didn't go. Then on the second day of their strike, a few Germans showed up with police dogs and they picked out a barracks. These barracks had two doors, one on each side. Then they sent these police dogs into the barracks. I'll tell you, those poor Russians were jumping out of windows or anything they could do to get out of there. Then finally, after they had done their job, one of the dogs came out, but after the Germans waited for the longest time, the other one never showed. So the Germans didn't know what happened to that dog.

We had these outhouses, great big, long, huge outhouses. Every week the Germans would send in these suction trucks to suck out all the shit out of these outhouses and then take it away so the local farmers could use it to spread on their fields as fertilizer. Finally, this one suction truck got clogged up and it couldn't suck up anything. Here the Germans found out that the Russians had killed the one dog, skinned it, and threw the hide in the latrine. That's what had clogged up the suction truck.

Oh, were those Germans ever mad. Those Russians were dead men. They were carrying out three or four dead men from their barracks a day. Every morning. They starved them. Oh, they took a beating.

The entire experience of being a POW still causes me to suffer until this day. I suffer with the effects still today. I can't sleep at night. War movies really get to me. I can't watch them. Then this war in the Gulf stirred everything back up for me. I'm just a nervous wreck right now. I try to forget it, but I just can't do it. Too much happened.

When our planes were bombing the Iraqis, it brought back memories of when our own planes bombed the hell out of us in Munich. There was a real big railway center there, and our guys bombed the hell out of it.

We lost 14 GI POWs when our own bombs fell on them. We just couldn't get out of the area fast enough. And the civilians. Oh, they did a number on them. Our guards made us clean up the site. We were picking up heads and arms, all kinds of things, for a long time. It was one big mess. You just can't forget this kind of stuff.

Another time, while I was still on the front line, there was a big forest, and on the other side of the forest was a big open field and we had a big battle there. Then, finally, we made our opening and were able to advance. Then when we got to the edge of the forest there was a lot of dead Germans. This one German was sitting there and he didn't look right to me. So I kicked him to try and roll him over and to see if he was alive, and he was. Then this German reached in his jacket pocket. I thought he was pulling a gun on me. What was I to do? I wasn't taking chances, so I killed him. But, afterwards, when I checked out what he was reaching for, I found out that he was just trying to show me a picture of his wife and two children [crying]. You take in all this stuff and it just stays with you. It never leaves.

Tom Grove

Tom Grove joined the clergy and then became a chaplain as the result of his experience as a POW.

I was a senior in high school, age 17. World War II was raging then, and I had an older brother who volunteered for the U.S. Army and was sent to North Africa. I was emotionally moved about him being there. The U.S. inductive services were speaking at high schools, motivating young men to go to the armed forces. I volunteered to go into the U.S. Army on January 16, 1943, the day I became 18.

We could sign up and get what branch of service we wanted. Well, I signed up for the air corps and got the infantry. On March 3, I was inducted and sent to Camp Wheeler, Georgia, for basic training. From there, we went straight overseas with no furlough. We went from Camp Wheeler up through the States and over into Washington state, got on a boat, and ended up in the Aleutian Islands, in Alaska and Dutch Harbor.

I got attached to an anti-aircraft outfit. Those soldiers had already been on the island about three years, so after about 14 more months they got to come back to the States, and I came with them. We who were there only 14 months got weeded out pretty quick. I ended up in Texas and got reassigned to Fort Jackson at Columbia, South Carolina. It was there that I got assigned to the 87th Division, the 345th Infantry. They were making preparation for overseas duty. We trained there for a period of time, then were shipped off to Camp Kilmer, New Jersey, for overseas duty again. With about 15,000 other soldiers, I boarded the Queen Elizabeth and sailed the Atlantic for the European Theater of Operations. After a short time in England, we boarded LST flat-bottom boats and crossed the English Channel.

We landed in France around October. It was well after D-Day, and we went in through Metz, France.

I saw my first dead soldier at Metz, France. It was a real scary thing. They were just laying all over the place. I can't express the horrible fears that I had. It was inexpressible. My vocabulary just doesn't hold the words. It was devastating, even though they were Germans.

After that, we became engaged in some real combat fighting. A couple of the places got real scary. One day the town we fought in belonged to the Germans, the next day it belonged to us. I got hit this one night when we were in a building. Now, as I look back, it was a barn, but we were fighting from house to house. There were German soldiers all over the place, and it was dark. As I backed up in this big room, something hit me and knocked me clear across the room. Later I found out it wasn't a German soldier. It was a horse that kicked me right in the lower part of the spine called the coccyx. It really knocked me down. And I couldn't get back up. It just about finished me. But because of self-preservation I knew I had to keep going, so I did. A few days later, we were in a place called Bonarue, Belgium, and there is where all hell broke loose.

The whole town was on fire. The German tanks were surrounding us, and here we were with just machine guns and rifles. It was hell on earth, combat all night long.

We held firm, but things really got rough. We were in this one house, my machine gun was set up in the bedroom window, in the upper story of a house. One German tank came around and pointed his cannon right toward the back window and pulled the trigger and the whole wall fell in. That's when my buddies got it. There was nothing left of them. They just disintegrated. Gone.

I was beside myself, but I had to keep alert. Then the same tank came around to the other side of the house and pointed his cannon up to the window where I was sitting with my machine gun. I knew I was gone— this was the last. I was so scared that I was afraid that my heartbeat was making too much noise. Had he seen me he would have just pulled the trigger. But I was just back far enough so he couldn't see me. However, I could see him and he had that tank cannon pointed right up at the window where I had my gun. All I could think was, this was it. It was soon going to be all over for me. The feelings of facing death were indescribable. I wouldn't classify myself as a real religious guy, but I believed in God, and I was praying. While frozen in place, I was so terrified that I just kept watching that gun on the tank. Then one of our guys that was still alive in the house began yelling for someone who knew how to use a bazooka. Bob, my gunner partner from Ohio, volunteered. He went down into the basement to try and get a clear shot at the tank. Before the bazooka could fire, the German tank fired his cannon into the basement area where a number of GIs were. Some were killed, others wounded. Those of us who were left scrambled out of the house as quickly as we could. Just as we got out, the tank shot another round. No more house. We just kept going from house to house. I had to leave my machine gun and run, so all I had to fight back against this tank was my 45 pistol.

We were just scrambling around like a bunch of ants. Then, finally, we got into a house, out of which a German 88 had blown out the whole back. My ammunition bearer panicked and said, "They're not getting me," and ran out through the back of the house. The German infantry that was accompanying the tank just mowed him down. And they just kept mowing him down until he moved no more. Then a sergeant named Williams decided to take the same route. "They're not getting me either," he yelled, and ran right through the same hole into the gun fire. Bless his heart. They took him down, too. However, he was lucky enough to be able to crawl back to safety. He was bleeding all over the place. The blood was popping right out of his legs where he had been hit. It was a horrible, horrible sight. The white snow was becoming red with blood. We were completely surrounded. If we tried to get out the back, we'd get German burp guns. If we went out the front, tanks and machine guns would mow us down. We decided that we were just going to play it cool and stay right there. In those last minutes, I told Ralph, "I don't want them to come and see me with a 45 pistol," because they would know that I was a machine gunner, and the word was that if you were a machine gunner, they would just finish you.

I didn't want to be captured as a machine gunner, so I took my ammunition belt off, cartridge belt, and anything else that would have given them a clue that I was a gunner and threw it all over the place. Then we decided to just play it defensively. If they throw a potato masher [German grenade] in, which is the norm, I said to Ralph I would pick it up and throw it out the hole. That was our last strategy as we awaited the end. Moments later, the Germans came to the front door and started talking in German. We just stayed quiet, expecting a potato masher, but it didn't come. They came in instead. They started talking German to us, and didn't shoot us, so I survived to tell the story. I was horrified when they took us outside. They took what personal items they wanted from us. Ralph was right beside me. He was about 6'2". As he put his hands about his head they took his watch. They took whatever they wanted. One SS German started to take my boots. I talked broken German to him and I said, by making signs with my hands and my feet, that mine were too small for his large feet. I talked him out of taking my boots. Still my feet got frozen in that sub-zero temperature. That was on January 6, 1945. I was with the 87th Division, 345th Infantry before being captured. I can remember most vividly that the Germans took us through this one wooded area which led to one of the most devastating feelings of my life. There our guys lay—our own American GIs—dead and all over the place.

We just had to keep walking, but as we did so I spotted this GI lying in a foxhole. He looked like he was sleeping, or at least my anger over the whole scene forced me to want to believe that. I was just hoping that he would pop out of his hole, mow down a couple of these Germans, and set us free. But it was just a hope, a hopeless dream. Your mind plays funny tricks on you like that when it's devastated, in shock. It's a horrible, inexpressible feeling. I was real tough, you know, 19 years old, and all full of fight when I first got over there, but you lose all that real quick when you hit the battlefield, endure what we endured, and see what we saw and experience what we experienced. But you just had to keep going. Your own survival was all that now mattered, after you got over the anger of wanting to kill these bastards for mowing down your buddies.

But once that leaves, a different type of trauma sets in. When they lined us up there, I can still remember, as if it were just yesterday, I said, "Oh my God, we are prisoners of war."

We all had to put our hands up over our heads. When they took what they wanted from us, they force-marched us. Because of the devastation we felt, each day's march felt about like five days. The further we were marched back in through Belgium and Germany, the more I really thought we were losing the war. Things just looked so bad. So many GIs and equipment captured.

I said to this one guy, "Let's try to escape." So we dropped to the end of the line and there were a couple of other guys really having a rough time keeping up. They could hardly walk, and often they fell. The Germans beat them with rifle butts. Then and there I made up my mind that I wasn't going to drop out of line. We kept being marched day after day, never being given anything to eat.

The first food we saw along the roads were frozen turnips which were red on the outside and white on the inside. We began jumping out of line to grab them but the German soldiers would shoot right at you, and just for going after a little food in the fields along the road.

We just kept marching and marching, all the way into Germany, sleeping in barns, if you were lucky, and living off whatever rotted food they could spare you.

Finally, some of us got assigned to forced labor in the German Army. They made us do all kinds of work. We were with an armored outfit, and we did all their labor work, whatever they didn't want to do. They captured a lot of U.S. Army equipment. At one particular time, they had us unload U.S. 30-caliber machine guns, which they had captured. We were unloading them from one big truck. I said to one American soldier, "You watch, and hand me the guns, and I'll take the firing pins out."

We didn't get caught. They made us carry this stuff up to a supply dump at the end of the road that they were making.

Still angry, I said to the same GI, "Let's blow up the ammunition dump whole. If it means we sacrifice ourselves, we'll take the whole outfit with us."

We looked for ways to blow up this ammunition dump and the Germans with all their equipment. We never could get the things planned out to do it. That's where I was in my feelings. I just knew this was the end.

During this time we were doing forced labor for this German outfit, I got caught between two vehicles. We were loading some kind of big equipment. I got pinned between two German trucks. It just about killed me. The Germans laughed and laughed because I was pinned between these two pieces of heavy equipment. I don't know what it was. I can't remember. I just kept screaming for my life. Finally the vehicles came apart and I just dropped to the ground, wrenching my lower spine, chipped my coccyx which still hurts me to this day whether I stand, sit or lay down. This injury I will take to the grave.

They would have been happy if I had been killed. They were so merciless. Some German soldiers that captured us looked as young as 15, and those were the soldiers that would come and stick their rifle right in your neck. They were called the SS troopers.

Finally, when we were out of this forced labor, we marched again for a number of days to our first prison camp. As we got in there, it looked like a big factory, not much of a roof left on it. It was all bombed out. It snowed right in on you. They gave each of us one little armload of straw which we used as our bed on the cold, wet floor. They fed us once a day with one piece of bread and some kind of lukewarm, watery tea.

What a devastating experience and horrible feeling, to see a thousand American soldiers there, and you were all helpless, just sweating it out, day by day by day. Then they put us in French 40-and-eight boxcars, which means 40 men or eight horses. They placed 86 of us in each car. That jammed boxcar became our kitchen without food, living room with no furniture, our bathroom with no facilities. Then the train got strafed by our own planes, and that is when you found out who the religious guys were, and those who weren't instantly became so. All these GI's including myself, just sat there singing "Nearer My God to Thee," "The Old Rugged Cross," all these hymns, while the bombs exploded outside and the machine gun bullets ripped hole after hole in the boxcars. We stayed in those things for five days. From there we were forced again to march, and we kept marching back into Bad Orb, Germany, which was the second POW camp I was placed in. During this time, I really began to get starved out.

One time I remember that we marched through some town. A lady had a slice of bread and just held it out for someone. I happened to go by at that moment and got it. I had a slice of bread that day, my best meal in a long time. We stayed in barns, but just kept on marching during the days. One night while sleeping in a barn, we milked a cow and got a little bit of milk. Finally we got to this last camp. They gave us a little piece of bread (one-seventh of a loaf), and watery potato soup. Actually, it was just warm water. If you were lucky enough to find a shred of potato skin, it looked like a T-bone steak to your starving eyes. And that was our diet until we got liberated.

When I got out of the POW camp, I weighed about 90 pounds. I went into the service at around 125 to 130 pounds. I was skin and bones when I came out.

We had lice all over us. Wherever your clothes were wrinkled, you would just shake them and kill lice by the thousands. The lice were so heavy that every place on your body that had hair was white with lice.

But the lack of food was the worst. One time these two GIs got so hungry that they went into this main building to steal food. And when they got in there, this one guy panicked, because his foot was apparently seen by a German guard. They attacked this German. In desperation and starvation, they about killed him, but they got away. So what the Germans did when they discovered this beaten guard was to line us all up and put their machine guns on us. They were going to kill us until the guys who were responsible for beating up the guard stepped forward. Finally, the two stepped forward. I'm sure they never got out of there alive. They just shot 'em.

Finally, we were liberated by the 43rd Division, right at the end of the war. They came in with tanks and tore down the wire fence surrounding the camp. We kissed those tanks just like they were American blondes and hugged the American soldiers who rescued us. The medical people looked at the food we were scheduled to eat that day and threw it out, saying it was not fit to eat. We reacted immediately, wanting to kill them because they were taking our food. That's how hungry we were. Then the Americans brought in C-rations. Without having any real food in our stomachs for months and because of our already weakened physical conditions, we all got stomach poisoning. Then dysentery set in. Wow! What a mess. This green stuff would just fly out of you. The whole prison camp became a latrine. Finally they brought in ambulances and took us out. We went through a hospital line and threw all of our clothes in a big pile which became a bonfire to burn them. They gave us one little bag to put whatever personal articles we had to keep. Then they gave us scrub brushes and sprayed us all for lice. After that, we just threw on whatever clothing they gave us. Size didn't matter.

We were then flown back to France to a camp called Lucky Strike, where they started rehabilitating us. We were there for a few weeks. They kept feeding us eggnogs and anything to try to fatten us up. Then they put us on a boat, and we went back to good old U.S.A. Seeing the Statue of

Liberty was a very tearful and emotional experience—free at last. We were now delivered and free. Each of us was granted a 60-day furlough. I really don't believe they knew what to do with this large group of liberated soldiers. I can now accept this wild, terrible, and traumatic experience, but I couldn't for a long, long time. Now I accept life as a gift of grace, that when all those guys around me went down, and to think, "Why not me?"

I've had so many emotional feelings. Even though I have accepted the experience, I haven't yet released it. I'm still in the process of doing that. But as I said, I can handle it a little better now, and I am glad that I can relate this today without a wall of emotion. I speak at a lot of Memorial Day programs in the county here, and then I speak at a number of churches on my own. But the entire experience is bothersome to me. I get so far and then as I begin to relate some experiences, I just fall apart, like I'm beginning to do now. I don't know what is happening to me, but the more I am getting it out, the more I am accepting what has really happened.

The toughest thing about being captured was that you had no control over your life whatsoever. They controlled it. You were under their domination. I was their slave. Whatever they wanted me to do, I did it, or else. And that was what was most devastating, working as one of their slaves. During those months, I never heard any other POW talking of loving up his wife or something like that, or going back and having an affair with some girl. Women, wine, and song are all very interesting, but not to a starving man.

I kept a little notebook. What I wrote about, dreamt about was what I was going to eat at my first meal. This is the kind of stuff we would talk about. One of us would say, "well I'm going to start my first breakfast with a quart of orange juice. Then I'm going to have a box of shredded wheat or Post Toasties. After that I'm going to have a dozen of eggs, a pound of bacon and two or three dozen pancakes."

That was going to be the first breakfast. This is what we talked about all the time.

The pressure to survive was always intense. In fact, there were some that just folded. In the second prison camp, spinal meningitis broke out. GIs just started dying like flies. We would just wrap them up in blankets and bury them. You just kept wondering if you were next. I can remember Easter Sunday saying I just wish I had what my dog is eating today, or I just wish I was back in America eating out of some garbage can. Now that just pops straight out of my mind. Today I can't really believe this story really occurred. It all seems like a bad dream or a TV program I watched. It's unbelievable to me today.

Those prisoner-of-war pictures on TV, I don't even watch them much. This "Hogan's Heroes." We never had that kind of shelter, food, or liberty. We were incarcerated: no food, no heat, no clean clothing, no nothing.

When I watch TV programs such as "Hogan's Heroes," it is disgusting to me. Even the war pictures. For when I go to bed afterwards, it all starts again. I begin to feel it, to relive it all. Yet in all senses, I'm kind of glad for the entire experience, even for all the pain it's caused and still is causing. I just wouldn't have the deep, deep appreciation for freedom that I do today if it were not for the experience. I wouldn't have the appreciation of the freedom that I enjoy, just being an American. I am just so glad just to be free. To walk out of a room into another room and go someplace else or just to be free. That is something. The experience makes me have an appreciation for freedom which I have never had. And I am not a big eater to this day even though I almost starved to death. You can tell that by looking at me. But I appreciate every morsel I have. And I can get along on very little and then I wonder, do I get along on little food because of the past experiences? I don't know.

But as far as the experience, how I have reacted, I never have really faced that question so direct until you put it to me. But now, I look back and I think, my God, I was spared for something. When I came back to the States by the way, I was living a pretty wild life—women, wine and song. Drunk a lot of the time. I was running around like crazy for about a year and a half. Then, like you hear, out came the old prodigal son. And the Lord began to become real to me. Then my lifestyle began to change. All of a sudden, I found myself going back to college. After graduation I felt directed toward ministry, so I went to seminary. After the Lord began to be real to me, I began to be able, for the first time, to look at, then accept what had happened to me. Now my story is starting to resurface more and more to me, and I am getting out these horrible feelings that I have had locked up in there for many years. I have been wonderfully amazed. Usually when I speak about this subject, I just go to pieces. Things just touch me so deeply and emotionally. When I see the American flag even in a parade, I just get all choked up, and I have emotional experiences. I remember how glad I am to be free, the buddies of mine that died over there, how lucky we are to be Americans.

Out of this entire episode of my life has evolved the entire focus of my existence, with God, with other POWs. I've begun working with them, sharing with them. I learn so much by being with them. So much of myself is brought out. So much has been allowed to be examined, understood, and then shared. It has been great therapy for me. For I've had some real difficult times emotionally. I don't mean that I needed to come to an institution, but just that I am bothered by a lot of different things in my life. I think it was post-traumatic stress that I was experiencing. And I didn't even know it. I just couldn't put some stuff together. But now coming into VA and doing clinical pastoral ministry, I have more understanding of myself and these ex-prisoners of war.

At the POW meetings, these ex-POWs get emotional when they talk about it. I thought I was sort of freaking out when I became emotional. I said to my wife, "I think I am abnormal."

These guys, remember the Iranian thing, that were captured in Iran. They came back, and they talked on TV and all. I couldn't have done that. I thought that something was wrong with me, for when I talked about my experiences, I'd just crumble and fall apart.

I spoke at a big American rally in July. The theme was on freedom. I was asked to speak on what freedom meant to me, and all of a sudden, I began having all of these experiences, and then I lost it. I felt terribly embarrassed. I didn't fully realize how much all this had affected me. That's why I'm coming in here every week doing clinical training to understand myself and these other veterans.

So much of what I have learned through this experience, so much of what I have become has helped me grow in my ministry. I will tell you what has happened to me. In this last year, I have been making a transition in my life. After 30 years in the parish ministry, I am in a transition as a result of my experiences and all that I've learned. It just has worked and worked on me so. At the present time, I am moving to the chaplaincy ministry so I can deal more with the individual person, like I do here at the vets' hospital in my work with ex-POWs. I'm so excited about that.

I presently spend two days of my time here each week in the hospital. And as I minister, of course, I am training and learning how to be a qualified hospital chaplain. After I finish training here in March, I am going to a residency program for one year, and that means full time. So I will resign at my church at that time and actually be assigned to a hospital, where I would minister all week, 40 hours while still training, and doing clinical work. After a year of clinical education, I'll have all the qualifications, and the academics, and the experience to be a chaplain. My goal is to be able to help some of these POWs, with the type of stuff they've helped me with, through my support of them. I would consider it a privilege to do so. I have a good feeling down here that I am able to relate to these elderly ex-POWs in the group. There are just so many of them out there, like 90,000. Most are really floundering. They haven't been able to find themselves, to come to know, experience, and turn themselves over to the delivering power of the Lord. And that is what I do today. I relate with great appreciation and feeling that we are all incarcerated today by sin, and if you let Him, God is able to come along now and free you, just like the 3rd Division came along and freed all of us from the POW camp. God is able to do that for anyone if we just trust Him. While there was nothing I could do in that camp about my actual deliverance, so there is nothing I can do today for my spiritual deliverance, only to trust in and turn to God, our Great Deliverer.

What I believe is that we are all incarcerated in one way or another. But God, just like the 3rd Division with us in the war, is just sitting outside our gates if we would only let Him in to free us. That message, to me, is my privilege to have worked so hard for in my life to be able to share. God is able to come in and give deliverance. My realization of this truth has made me a new person.

For before I came upon this realization, I wasn't any different from most of the guys—angry. I just couldn't seem to put anything together. I was always cussing in my mind, in my memories at those dirty German bastards, as I saw them. I just didn't have anything together. My life was scattered and fragmented. But that is all different today, for I have let God in that front gate and He has freed me of my past and of the pains of myself.

If I could change it all, go back in time, I'd just as soon go back to Germany, back to Stalag 9B where I was, and I would tell what has happened to me. I would live that. I really would. Then I look around me and I see all my comrades that were POWs in the war, and they are still locked up. Some won't even talk. They were initially imprisoned 45 years ago, and still haven't left their cells. They don't even know there's a way out.

I was just speaking with one ex-POW before you came in. He is so reluctant to open up. He just wants to keep all the pain out of his mind. Thus, he holds it all in. He doesn't share it, so he can experience freedom and understand it. He is scared to step outside the cell which he has built for himself. There is so much freedom to be found if one lets it out. Holding it in is what is standing between them and their true selves, and freedom. When I was in their shoes, I didn't even know I was locked up either. That's the toughest part, realizing that you are imprisoned.

Actually, we were all locked up with sin before we even left for the war, but our incarcerations just furthered our frights to be able to step out and go in search of our real selves to find God. That's why it's been so much harder for us, but yet maybe even more exhilarating for us once we are finally freed. And it doesn't matter what age one gets that freedom. Freedom is freedom. It's our goal here and our purposes to acquire as children of God.

Such is the most important understanding any of us can make. That's why I feel God has led me here to these guys. I am one of them. I can talk to them straight out, no academics, no college, Greek, or Hebrew stuff, just the truth. And I can relate to them and their conditions because I am one of them. Allowing God to work through me like this, I can make a difference, help release these men from the type of cell I was also locked away in for so long, so they can finally find the freedom that God has awaiting them.

PART THREE

THE JEWISH POW

It would be remiss to write a book on the experience of the American POW of World War II without including a section on the treatment of the Jewish-American prisoner of war by the Germans. In a vast number of cases and nearly until the conclusion of the war, the treatment of the Jewish POW was no different from that of the non-Jew, as evidenced in the first of the following three interviews. But one glaring exception does exist, and that deals with the removal and transfer of 350 American POWs, approximately 150 of whom were Jews and the remaining 200 of whom the Germans thought to be Jews, from a prisoner-of-war camp named Bad Orb to the death camp Berga-Elster. There is some evidence that the Germans, in a last-minute, desperate effort, were planning to exterminate all Jewish-American POWs near the end of the war, as suggested by the two recollections that follow this one. These two stories speak for themselves.

Peter Neft

Peter Neft, a cocky, Jewish pilot, was never affected by any end-of-the-war plot to eradicate Jews. The worst thing that happened to him was that he, along with almost every Jewish-American POW, was segregated from his non-Jewish comrades in January 1945, which may or may not have been part of the plot mentioned. But for all relevant purposes, he grew from the extreme conditions he survived through.

Because of the friendships I made, the fellowships of other POWs, the helping each other, that experience, we keep helping each other, a group of POWs is like a big, happy family. We may have disagreements, minor disagreements, but we are friends. Even though we aren't from the same camp, we don't know each other, we still share the same experience. We have a bond between us.

Now I'll tell you how I happened to become a POW. It was January 29, 1944. I was a co-pilot on a B-17. We were supposed to bomb Frankfurt that day. As luck would have it, we were assigned a plane from another squadron, not our regular airplane. And we took off and proceeded on with our group to Frankfurt, and just as we dropped our bombs, one of our engines went out. The prop could not be feathered. Anyone not in the Air Force probably doesn't know what that means. The plane would normally fly on three engines, but if you can not feather the bad engine, it slows the airplane down considerably. We became a straggler and we drifted back out of formation. The German fighters jumped us. Exactly what happened, happened so quick I couldn't see it. Believe me, I saw German fighters, and that was it. I asked the flight engineer to transfer the gas from the bad engine into the other good engine. There was a procedure for doing that, which he proceeded to do. The just as we did that, the fighters attacked us. I looked back and saw him sitting on the floor of the turret, and I said, "Reel, get back in the turret."

He said, "We have no turret. The fighter attack sheared it off."

Fortunately, he was not in the turret when it happened.

We then decided to dive down to a layer of clouds, which was 5,000 or 6,000 feet. We put the plane into a steep dive. The fighters followed us all the way down, taking pot shots at us. We finally leveled the plane off and headed back for England. We were limping along with the damaged plane popping out of the clouds every once in a while. We got about 50 miles from the Channel coast.

I then called the radio operator and told him to notify the air/sea rescue of our position in case we had to ditch in the Channel, but he told me that the fighter attack had destroyed everything. Everything went along real fine until we lost our cloud cover and we were left out in the open.

A couple of German fighters jumped right on us and set us on fire. We decided it was time to bail, for once a plane is burning, it is a very dangerous situation.

Well, the pilot and I went back into the bomb bay where we were supposed to bail out. The procedure is that the pilots, radio and flight engineers go out the bomb bay. The waist and tail gunners go out the waist, and the bombardier and the navigator go out the nose. But when we got to the bomb bay, the radio operator and the flight engineer refused to bail out. They thought we were over water at the time because we had drifted back into the clouds, and the pilot couldn't convince them differently. So he turns and says to me, "You go first, I'll be right behind." So I jumped out with him following right behind.

I landed safely on a field. After I got unhooked, I threw my chute and everything away and took off for a nearby patch of woods. Then I heard a voice calling to me from behind me in the distance. When I turned around, I saw two German soldiers pointing rifles at me, gesturing me to surrender. Which I did by throwing up my hands and walking toward them. I turned over my 45 automatic and they put me in the sidecar of their motorcycle and drove to the little town that was a garrison.

Unfortunately, no one at the garrison could talk English, but I could understand German. They then told me that they were going to take me to another village where they had a garrison also. There was a sergeant that spoke fluent English.

The strangest thing happened to me on the way there. While they were loading me into one of their military Volkswagens, the guard who was trying to climb into the back seat with me was having a difficult time doing so because of his machine pistol. So he handed it to me to hold for him. There it was in my hands and I just sat there looking at it and saying to myself, "Good grief." The other soldier reached over me and took it out of my hands.

Then they took me to this German master sergeant. He asked me my name, rank, serial number, all the usual routine questions. Then he asked me if I was hungry, and I said yes, that I was. I hadn't eaten since morning. I was served a nice dinner on white table linen. An enlisted man served the dinner. It was the best meal I had in a year. Then they took me to an air base. He said the war is over for me, that I am very lucky to still be alive and not even wounded. He then told me that I would be sent to a POW camp where I would live the life of Reilly. He left shortly after and I was left only in the company of a few guards to watch over me. Then one of the guards handed me a hunk of black bread and said, "This is your ration for the day." I looked at that and I said to myself, "Am I going to live on this for the rest of the war?"

Then they put me in the cell. The Germans were very nice, by the way. They were friendly. They showed me how their weapons worked and everything. Then they brought in some German who gave me a lecture about the atrocities I committed against the German people. Afterwards they put me in the cell and locked me up. All I had in there, and it was January, to keep we warm was a little stove that worked well if you could keep it lit.

Later that day, they brought in my radio operator and flight engineer, the two who had initially refused to bail out. But because they had bailed out when the plane was so low, they had each broken a leg. The German guard asked me if I would mind switching cells with them because my cell was already heated and warm, the other cell wasn't. And I said no, that would be fine. That carried a lot of weight with the German guard because they had a lot of respect for an officer, even though their officers treated them like dirt. Yet, here I was, an officer, giving up my warm cell to my two sergeants with broken legs.

Shortly afterwards, when I discovered that I could reach outside my cell and slide the deadbolt on my door off, I started to think about escaping. Later that night, I worked up the courage to make my attempt. So I reached outside the window opening in my door and slid the deadbolt over, opened the door, and closed it behind me. Once outside I started out cross-country until I ran into a canal, and I started to move along up its banks, where I finally ran into a sentry post located on the opposite side. The sentry must have heard me moving through the brush or something because he began yelling in my direction. He then touched his flashlight over toward me, but I just kept moving. He yelled a couple more times and I still kept going until he picked up his rifle and slid a cartridge into the firing chamber and pointed it in my direction. Well, I still didn't figure it was worth dying for.

Up I came out of the brush like a jack-in-the-box, and I figured they would be pretty mad at me for escaping, but they weren't. They just joked about it. It was a big laugh to them, but they made sure I couldn't get out of the cell again. They put a padlock around the deadbolt. The next day they took me to a military prison.

En route they stopped to pick up this German captain, typical Prussian type, the kind you see in the movies, arrogant, dressed perfectly, not a wrinkle in his clothing. I was dirty and muddy. Then the captain told the sergeant to sit in the front with the driver who was a private. In other words, being an officer he would not sit with the sergeant. If he had only known that here I was, not only dirty and muddy and the enemy, but Jewish to boot.

They took us to this military prison, and I was locked up for two days. It was an awful place. Again the guards were not abusive or anything. There was this German prisoner in the next cell to me who was very friendly. His girlfriend had brought him some cake and he split it with me. After that they took me to Frankfurt where they had what they called the *Dulag*, which is a transit camp for ranking personnel where they put you in solitary confinement for a few days, question you, and then put you in another part of the camp. And when they had enough to make a shipment, they shipped you up to a regular prison camp. I don't know how long I spent there. Over a week. I was there for two air raids, and I remembered that I had been given the information before we bombed there that Frankfurt was going to be leveled, wiped off the map, by the 8th Air Force. They were not going to hit it every day, but take a more deceptive approach. Frankfurt one day and another place the next. Then back to Frankfurt. Then on to another place. But always Frankfurt.

After being in Frankfurt, they shipped us north to the Baltic Sea, to Stalag Luft I, where they were testing and firing their rockets. We could see it from our camp. It was there that they discovered I was Jewish. It was on my dog tag. I, unlike so many others, didn't make any attempt to hide it. I was cocky. All of us pilots were. We were the best the United States had to offer, and we knew it. We had volunteered for duty. About 10 percent of the guys that volunteered to be pilots didn't even pass the interview. Another 25 percent didn't pass the physical. Twenty percent of who were left didn't pass the mental tests. Out of who was left, only maybe half made it through the flying tests. Only, at best, 10 percent of those who volunteered to be pilots actually made it. Thus, we were cocky. We didn't care what Hitler was doing to the Jews. We weren't going to back away from who we were. We were crazy. Three guys that I roomed with were Jewish also, and they didn't keep it a secret either. In fact, we were so cocky that we began holding Jewish services. So one of our guys, an Englishman, removed the cross from the camp chapel on Saturdays and replaced it with a Star of David so we could use the space to have a service of our own. We were crazy.

The Germans didn't seem to care about us being Jewish till one day, early in January in 1945, they made up a list of all the POWs that were

Jewish, asked us to pack up our belongings, and moved us out. Well, that is when I really got scared. They moved us to another part of the camp. We were in a barracks by ourselves. We even had a Jewish sergeant with us that acted as our orderly. That was their policy. Every barracks just had so many sergeants assigned to it as orderlies for the officers. The English officers in the camp and the American officers, except for maybe the colonels and the high rankers, did that. We were just lieutenants, and we didn't go for that stuff. But nevertheless we had 12 sergeants. All they had to do was sweep the hall. But they were supposed to do everything. All they did was sweep down the hall once a day, though, which wasn't a big job, and everything was fine. Their jobs were easy. There was nothing wrong with the barracks. Ours were not as crowded because of our situation. We figured it was either to show that they weren't mistreating, or the other way around. The Germans didn't have the transportation, since they were cut off to the south, to move us out. And if they got moving us out, every guard would have been killed anyway. That I know for a fact. That is the part of the story that I like the best. Talk about POWs helping each other. When I moved out of the other compound, my roommate, we had all been hoarding a little food. We had a nest egg built up because we thought the day would come when nothing would come in. They each slipped extra food that they had been saving into mine. They needed it just as bad as I did. We were all hungry. They did that for me. I will never forget it. Like I say it, after 15 months we could hear the Russian Army coming in the distance, the artillery. See, our camp was on what is now the Communist side of the block. As the Russians started to cut across the base of the peninsula, the Germans wanted to move the whole camp. Colonel Zempke, who was our senior officer, said we wouldn't go. They couldn't control 10,000 men, especially with the amount of guards they had and especially because the guards were senior citizens, what you would call third-line troops. So they moved out without us. A couple of days later, the Russian Army showed up. After the Germans left, we just waited around to be rescued and feasted on the food the Germans had stored in a warehouse. When the Russians arrived, there was nothing they wouldn't do for us, especially the Americans. They didn't like the English. But the Americans were their friends. And anything you asked them for, if they had it, they gave it to you. The Russian soldiers were very generous with what they had. They came in one day with a truck. Four or five of them. We all gathered around. We were curious. The first bunch that had come through was a guerrilla unit, but they moved on. Then the Mongols came in after them. They were short, with bandy legs. When they came into the camp, we all gathered round to see what their equipment was like. This one Mongol pulled out a big hunk of black bread and he started to give us all bread. He handed it to us fellows and then he pulled out a jug of wine and a cup. We were told that if they offer anything, don't refuse it, even if you don't want it. Don't refuse it. It would offend them. They offered us everything they had. So as I say, they were very nice and friendly.

I had been shot down on my fifteenth mission. You needed to fly 25 to be sent home. Most never flew more than five. I was one of the few who had 15 missions. Never thought I'd be shot down, or I never would have gone. Well, I didn't know that I was going to get shot down, but I got some stomach problems as the result of being a POW. I didn't know if it was malnutrition or what, but I have a restriction in my esophagus. I didn't get any disability for it from the government. It was too hard to trace it to my time as a POW for them to acknowledge it.

When I came out of the camp I weighed about 110 pounds; when I entered the Army I weighed 160. My Army fighting weight was 145. I lost most of my weight in the period of time from late December to mid-April. We called that the depression. We were getting practically nothing at all to eat, maybe a potato a day and three slices of bread, and occasionally some German margarine or cabbage soup, and that is all we had. In fact, my buddy and I agreed to share everything that we had. We made that agreement. He was pretty good with tools. He took a knife and sharpened it so you could cut the bread real thin. Our normal three slices weren't the same thickness as anybody else's, and we'd save a little. Over a period of time we accumulated a whole loaf of bread. And we got a hold of some German coffee. It was awful, but it was coffee. Then we got some German jam and margarine. You couldn't eat that bread raw. It was like sawdust. We made toast in the fire on the stove, and ate the whole loaf between us at one sitting.

One of the follows in the room wrote me a letter. He is in a small town in Louisiana. He said he had a copy of his diary and he wrote about the time we ate a whole loaf of bread. There wasn't much envy in our group. We were lucky. We sort of helped each other out. So nobody gave us a hard time about having all that bread. We had accumulated it, so it was ours and that was it.

There is another surprising thing. Even though I was Jewish, all my parcels came through regularly. My parents were allowed to send a parcel every two months, and I got a fruitcake. It was mailed for Christmas. But I didn't get it till after Christmas, during the period we called the depression. I was offered $300 for it. Of course, I didn't sell it. Leonard Rosen and I lived on that. Every day, we would slice off a thin slice. It was a miracle. I think that fruitcake helped us out for about two weeks. But I can't stand fruitcake now. But then it was food. And whenever we got food, we shared it. When you are in the position that we were in, you had to live with one another. You didn't try to take something. I wouldn't steal anybody's clothes or anything. The fact that you had something meant that you would share it. Cigarettes? I was getting more cigarettes than I ever needed. The chaplain was a Presbyterian minister. We got very friendly with him, and he told me that he was going to visit another camp and they didn't have any cigarettes. He asked me if I could spare some. I gave him six cartons. He said "Aren't you running yourself short?"

No. At that time I didn't smoke. I had so many cigarettes that I didn't have enough matches to light them all. Nobody died in our camp. Well, wait. There was one guy who got shot for stepping outside when there was an air raid.

Like I say, we were never abused. We were just hungry, mad. But we were never abused. It was all Air Force in our camp. We were treated just so much better than the infantry. First of all, ours was an officer's camp. Like I said, the Germans had a very high regard for officers. Suppose a German guard was going to deliver a message to somebody. He would knock on our door and wait until he was invited in. Then he would salute. So, as I said, they were very conscientious about that. We were officers, and they tried to live up to their obligations to us as that. I always felt that in Germany, the European caste system, only the aristocracy could become officers. But I don't think the aristocracy was the same. The SSers just used the brown shirts, always looked down on them. The SSers were not the aristocracy. But confinement, being cooped up, 14 or 15 people in one room, was the toughest part of being there. We had to get along. But still you do get on each other's nerves. But the experience was worth a million bucks. I could fill a book.

Now some fellows maybe they feel that they didn't get anything when they were in prison, and didn't make the most of it. But we made the most of it. In fact, one of our guys says that we acted crazy, but we had to to keep from going insane. We had a hell of a lot of fun when we were in prison. We did some crazy things. The Germans had a lot of respect for flying officers, we were seen as the elite too, real cocky. We won our silver wings, and we were.

In fact, we were treated better over there. Then, when we got home, we were degraded. People thought we had it too easy because we were in prison camp, with all the rationing they had at home and all. I was welcomed home with open arms by my immediate family, people that I was very close with. But everybody had it so tough during the war that they were always complaining about how rough they had it. They didn't want to hear what I had to say, so I just listened, and they thought I had it so easy as a POW. So I just started keeping away from those people. I don't regret what I did. I went in the Army. I don't like having been a POW, but if I had to do it over, I would do the same thing. In fact, my buddy Gordon stayed in the Army. He fought in Korea. He fought in Vietnam. Another buddy, Frank Upson, fought in Korea and Vietnam also. Those two I can speak for. I can't speak for anybody else.

I don't know if you are familiar with who the Army used to take as enlistments or not, but if you were a bad kid and too young to go to jail, they gave you a choice of going in the Army as long as you got two letters of recommendation. That is what a lot of the peacetime Army was made up of, especially the enlisted men.

I knew a guy who was peacetime Army. I couldn't get along with him. He was miserable. He hated Jews and made no bones about it. But after the POW experience, he changed. He was on the same ship that I came home on. One day I came down with what I imagined was the flu, but we had no medication. He came in the room and asked what was wrong with me. I was laying in bed all covered up. One of the guys told him I had the flu. He came back in about three minutes. He had some tablets. He said, "Take a couple of these, Pete. They may help you."

He stayed in the Army and he came through Pittsburgh on leave. He was a changed man. But when he first got in, he was the most miserable son of a gun that ever lived. Everybody hated his guts.

Before I got shot down, we didn't bomb Paris, but we did bomb a ball-bearing factory that was near Paris. We had a tough break there, too. We had a plane that broke down on us. It broke down before we dropped our bombs. We were flying about 30,000 feet. There was another group bombing at 25,000 feet. We couldn't drop our bombs, so we dove down and joined this other group, and dropped with them. Our navigator, he saw pictures of the bombs when they hit. A bunch of bombs must have been off the target. It must have been our bombs, he said.

We bombed rocket installations in France, too. Bordeaux was a long, tough one. We had about 90 minutes of a fighter attack. Flying at a high altitude is hard work. It's tough to keep in formation. You're all so close. We used to take turns, my pilot and I, 30 minutes on, 30 minutes off. I was flying one time and when my 30 minutes were up, Frank, my pilot, told me that he couldn't switch with me because we would drift too much. And since the group ahead of us was under fighter attack, we may get too far out of formation and because they were under attack and busy, they wouldn't be able to compensate. So we came in and we dropped our bombs on the airport. Usually the German fighters didn't follow us over water, but this time they did. Fortunately, we weren't hurt. We may have picked up a few bullet holes, but that is about all. That was the only time they ever followed us over water. The pilot's oxygen system went bad that time, too. That meant I had to take over until we got safely over the North Seas and then down to a lower altitude.

The time we bombed Kiel, now that was a time. I don't know what did it, but we heard an explosion in the cockpit at about 30,000 feet. I just looked at the pilot and he looked at me. When we got on the ground we still didn't know what happened. The first thing our crew chief did was go through the entire plane.

He said, "What happened to your windshield?"

"Why?" I asked. A bullet had come right through it. We didn't even know it. We heard it, but we didn't know what it was. But again, that didn't scare us or worry us, as long as it didn't hit us.

Before I got shot down, I knew that Hitler was liquidating the Jews. I got it like everyone else—from the Jewish news media. And Auschwitz had Jewish publications which we were privy to as well. Knowing that may have been one of the reasons I volunteered. I enlisted right at the post office in Pittsburgh. I was just under the wire as far as they were concerned. In fact, when I applied, I passed the physical, I passed the mental and then I talked to the captain.

He told me, "You will be notified. Your appointment to aviation will come through in a month or so."

I said, "Captain I don't have a month. I will be over the age limit in a month."

So he said, "I'll tell you what, you will be appointed just a day before your birthday," which was the truth.

The captain was nice enough. He came through. But I was like the senior citizen in the camp. Very few pilots were my age. I was 27 at the time. The cut-off had been 26. So I had my thirtieth birthday in the prison camp. In fact, my instructor in basic flying school wanted to recommend me for fighter pilot school.

I said, "I don't think I can make a fighter pilot."

"Why not?" he asked.

"My age," I said.

"How old are you?"

I told him. He couldn't believe it. Everyone assumes little, 'cause I was short, means young.

There was an escape attempt when I was a prisoner in the original barracks, before I was segregated. We used to exercise around the compound, just before it got dark, just walking mostly. I was walking with Stan Dolgin. He was the fellow I was talking about earlier. He was pretty smart. In fact, he was a brilliant man.

He says, "Pete, there is an attempted escape tonight."

I said, "Stan, how do you know?"

He said, "Take a look around. See all the majors and lieutenant colonels are wearing heavy sweaters under their jackets. What's more, the escape is going come out of our barracks."

I said, "What makes you think so?"

He said, "I just saw five or six of the big brass walking into our barracks. They don't live in our barracks."

Sure enough, we got to our barracks, walked into our room, and it was jammed.

And the lieutenant colonel said, "Keep your voices down, everybody, keep quiet. Get against the wall until the Germans lock the shutters."

And before you know it a couple of fellows started to rip up the floor. The tunnel was dug underneath our room, and we didn't even know it.

But the escape was called off because of an air raid, and during an air raid the Germans turned their dogs loose in a patch of woods where the tunnel was going to end.

So the colonel said, "You fellows here in this room, keep your mouths shut."

Which we did. Then the next day, we came in. We are all prepared. The brass was all there. We knew it was going to go out that day, so we opened the tunnel. Did you ever see the picture *The Great Escape*? They always dug the tunnel short. We did the same thing. When I saw that movie, I said, "Everybody digs it too short."

We were just past the fence. Not into the woods. That basically ended it. You saw a lot of confusion shortly after, and all hell broke loose. The Germans knew that the escape came from our room because we were right near the corner of the building. The first thing you knew, the shutters were opened up, and the German guards came in and they put a dog down to guard the hole in the tunnel. Everybody had crawled out of the tunnel by the time the guard came.

But that is when I was scared because their dogs were vicious. That dog just sat by that tunnel and nobody bothered him or bothered to even go near that hole. I just laid there in my bed with a blanket pulled up to my nose. Finally they took the dog out. Then they rounded up everybody in the barracks and sent them all to solitary confinement, but they only had so many solitary confinement cells. So some guys never did get to serve their sentence. I think they had about 60 to 70 guys lined up to try and escape that night. They found guys hiding in the rafters of the roof. That was in the summertime, of course, because it didn't get dark till late. Summertime is the only time you can escape because it is too cold otherwise.

I worked in the tunnel once. Stan Dolgin talked me out of it though.

He said, "Pete, you are crazy."

"First," he says, "do you talk German fluently?"

I said, "No."

Then he asked, "Do you have any maps?"

"No," I replied.

Next he asked, "Do you have any civilian clothes?"

"No," I replied again.

"When you get out of here, where are you going to go? If you look at the map, we're as deep in Germany as you could get. The only way out is to swim across the Baltic Sea. You're safe in this camp. You are Jewish. If the Germans catch you outside of this camp, if you get into the hands of the Gestapo, you are a dead duck."

He was right, so I stayed.

Bernie Melnick

Bernie Melnick is one of the approximately 90 American POWs who survived their two-month stay in Berga-Elster. Two articles in which Bernie was interviewed about Berga-Elster have been included in Appendixes B and D to give a more in-depth understanding of all that took place.

The notice came in around the 18th of January—my birthday is January 18, 1924, so it was around my twenty-first birthday—and the order was announced over the loudspeakers. All soldiers of Jewish faith were supposed to report that night to a certain segment of the camp.

The camp was in shock, 'cause we were all Americans. None of the guys saw each other through the eyes of a certain denomination or religion. We'd also heard for a long time what Hitler had been doing to the Jewish people. We didn't know that he had been exterminating them, but we knew of how the Jews had been mistreated before the war. We had read about how all their possessions had been taken from them; and during the war that they had been rounded up and sent to labor camps.

The Germans gave us the whole day to think about what was going to happen to us. They were cruel like that. I don't know if they meant it that way. But if they did, the tactic sure worked, because we were petrified.

Some of the Jewish guys had thrown away their dog tags when they had gotten captured so that the Germans wouldn't know that they were Jewish. Others just tried to hide the fact once they got in camp, and we never thought of pointing them out to the Germans or anything. Though most of the boys didn't try to hide where they came from or what they believed in. All that comes as part of being a Jew. Through the centuries, with all that we've been through, we've had to learn to be proud of who we were. Thus it was only natural for us to step forward. It was what being a Jew was all about.

Our camp wasn't any "Hogan's Heroes" though, and what we were experiencing and were about to go through was no joke. The Germans were no dummies. In fact, they were very smart and crafty.

But the entire camp reacted great. They were really behind us. Shortly after the announcement had come over the loudspeakers, guys began speaking up. The whole camp was behind us. There was no concern about what religion we were. We were all in this together. We were allies, Americans. Immediately, there was talk about how they could stop us from being taken, and how it was against everything in the Geneva Convention. There were talks of protests, escapes, revolts, everything. All the guys were 100 percent behind us.

But me and all the other Jewish boys that stepped forward realized that there wasn't much they could do for us. But that didn't stop them from turning out by the thousands to see us off. It was like a send-off of Olympic athletes; everyone was there to cheer us on. There must have been 3,000, maybe 4,000 guys. We marched right through the center of them, us and our German guards, all 50 of them. The Germans had sent in a higher number than would be usually needed to escort us out because the tensions were so high that they were scared to death of something happening. We marched proudly out of there as the guys cheered us on and jeered at the guards. The other soldiers' support for us meant more to us than we would ever be able to explain.

The Germans marched us right into the designated area and into our designated barracks, never once telling us why we had been segregated. Thus we had no conclusion at all why we were there. At first we all tried to talk about it, attempting to guess what we could be in for. Then eventually we all just laid there and wondered. We had no idea why we were there at all. Let me tell you, there were a lot of sleepless nights in our barracks that evening.

But we didn't have to wait too long. Because at six o'clock in the morning, the guards came in kicking the bottom of our beds and screaming, "Get out. Get out. Get out of the barracks."

We thought maybe they were going to shoot us or something. When we got outside, two other barracks of Jewish guys were already lined up outside, carrying their shoes. Some wore their clothes while others carried theirs. Some guys took along their paper-thin wool blankets, too. Some guys wore them over their heads to keep warm. Then two more other barracks emptied out into the grounds, and then another six, until a few hundred Jews were all lined.

But then, if you looked far enough down this long, long line of bodies, you could see at the farthest end 150 or so guys lined up with us that were non-Jews. I found out later that what had happened was that Hitler knew that the war was coming to an end for all was going bad for him. So he gave out some type of order to try and speed up the killing of all the Jews. I guess somewhere in his madness he also sent out orders to also start the killing of Jewish-American POWs. Supposedly, he sent out specific orders to all his commandants to begin doing such. Up until then Hitler had lost all control over his officers. Well, anyway, I guess it was Hitler's belief that out of every so many American POWs, a certain number were Jews, something like 10 percent. So when our commandant decided to follow Hitler's orders, he was responsible for accounting for a specific number of Jews. And since there were somewhere around 3,500 POWs in our camp, according to Hitler's percentage that meant there had to be 350 Jews. But there weren't anywhere close to that many, even if all of the Jews who had thrown away their dog tags and the ones who had just denied being Jewish had stepped forward. So the Germans began rounding up non-Jews just to fill their quota. "Undesirables," they called them. Supposedly they were guys that had caused problems before, troublemakers. But I later found out that this wasn't true as well. They just randomly herded in gentiles to suffer the same fate as us Jews. That's who those guys were at the end of the line that morning, gentiles who the Germans called undesirables. Guys that in just one way or another resembled Jews.

Twelve guards were stationed in front of us with machine guns and rifles pointed in our direction. A list was read off, kind of a roll call. Whatever information they needed from us was given to them and they took it down in minutes. Then they marched us out. Like I said, Germans are very efficient.

We were somewhat subdued and confused by the presence of all the gentiles. For at the time we didn't have the foggiest idea what was happening. We may have thought that we hadn't known much about what was going on the night before, but we knew even less the following morning.

We were marched right out through the main gate of the Stalag 9B camp, about 20 or 30 minutes down the hill, in the town of Bad Orb. Then we were trucked to a marshaling yard in a nearby town. It was a tremendous railyard, with between 100 and 150 boxcars sitting around, lined down the tracks, engine up ahead, puffing and steaming, waiting to choo-choo away as soon as the Americans were loaded aboard. Once we got to the railyard, the guards double-timed us to the end of the long transport, and counted out 50 of us for each boxcar and then forced us to go inside. Then the doors were shut, wired and latched behind us. The train started to pull out shortly after. It was obvious that all of this had been prearranged for quite some time. They were just so well planned out. And there we were, stuffed into these boxcars like cattle.

It took us four or five days to get to Berga, which was part of Buchen-wald, one of Hitler's main extermination camps. But along the way we were able to piece things together by what we saw. Because we were con-stantly getting strafed by American and British planes, we got to see a lot. When a boxcar was hit and completely shattered by an Allied bomb dropped, we were chosen to help remove all the bloody dead bodies. The boxcar contained civilians and was very near the end of the line of 100 or 150 boxcars. It looked like a vicious cowboy-and-Indian shootout. Out of six or seven of our boxcars, mine was unwired, unlatched, and every GI ordered out to gather dead and half-dead bodies for immediate burial in graves dug along the banks of the railroad tracks. In a matter of hours the GIs were back in the car and the train took off, east towards the Czechoslovakian border. But while we were outside the cars, we got to see a lot and gather some information as well. What we were able to discover was that we were typical shipment of Jews out of Frankfurt, bound for the camps.

But we didn't find out anything about Berga, which was Hitler's version of an extermination camp for Jewish-American POWs, until we arrived, and we really didn't find out much about it until we'd been there a while. The reason nobody could tell us anything about our role at the camp or what we were doing there was because we were the first and only American POWs to be put in such a position by the Germans.

When we got to Berga, we got out and lined up, and for the first time we got to fully see the hundreds and hundreds of non-servicemen, all Jews, we'd shared the train ride with. As we were lined up and marched away from the train station, we passed by, going in the opposite direction, a long line of skeletal-looking civilian men. Little did I know that by the end of my stay that would be me. From there we were marched to a makeshift stockade where six or seven barracks had been set up.

Our normal work routine started the next day. We were required to do the same work as the stronger Jewish civilian males in Buchenwald that they were trying to work all the life out of before gassing them. In fact, that may have also been another reason that our stockade had been set up so quickly and we had been shipped there. Hitler was simply doing such a good job at working the Jewish men to death that he was falling short on his labor force. Those Germans sure are efficient. So we were brought in so he could do the same to us. But he didn't know that only half of us were Jews, even though the work report he may have eventual-ly seen probably said so.

Our work routine was pretty simple to follow but hell to execute in our extremely deflated physical condition, and we weren't getting better, with the starvation diet we were on, as time went by. We passed the other pitiful-looking souls on the way into and out of the mines everyday. They were all inhabitants of Buchenwald. We were marched in in the morning and worked all day until the night, when they replaced us. This went on from mid-January until mid-April, when we were finally evacuated. There was never much eye contact or anything between they or us. At best, one got a blank stare. But most of the time we just walked by each other with our heads down. From a quick conversation while sharing a commode, I learned that one civilian, who said he was 45 years old (though he looked more like 70-ish), had been on this detail over four years. He claimed he was picked up in Prague and his clothing factory confiscated when the Nazis marched in. This brief encounter ended when the guards came to separate us, but not before I blurted to the civilian that I was drafted. By now I was fully aware of my Jewishness and more and more afraid to talk.

Since we were only a few miles away from the German lines in Czechoslovakia though, an escape attempt was always on our minds. That was until one day when four of our guys ran away on the way to the work site and headed toward Prague. They had only been gone a few days when the Germans brought them back into camp. They had been picked up only a few miles away. They were heading toward the Russian lines when the SS caught them and executed them. A detail was chosen to bring them back to camp on dollies. When the detail arrived back in camp the SS officers who had shot them in the heads dumped them on the ground in front of us.

"If anyone tries to run away," they told us, with the guys lying there dead on the ground, "you will be executed."

A detail was then chosen to take them into town and bury them. This may sound like a terrible job, and it was, yet everyone wanted to do it, because it gave you a chance to beg for food from the civilians on the way. One of the rare benefits was getting the deceased's shoes, if the SS didn't get them first. Thus guys were always eager to go. And with at least a guy or two a day dying in camp, there were plenty of details to get on. I myself never went through a man's pockets, but others helped themselves. You came to look at life differently. It was part of your life. Nothing else mattered. By then I was mostly out of my mind. I can't believe to this day I was like that.

Our guys were buried in some ground on the outside of a cemetery. If you could get a farmer to look at you you could then beg for food. We especially tried to get their attention when we'd momentarily leave the detail to piss or defecate.

At the gravesite we were allowed to say a prayer if we wanted to. But we were never allowed enough time or never had enough materials to erect a crucifix or a Star of David. There were about a 150 of us Jews at Berga and about another 200 gentiles. There were about another 20,000 political male prisoners in Buchenwald. They needed that many to get any work at all done because everyone of us was so weak and beaten down.

Guys were dying like flies. Some literally passed out and died as they walked either to or from the mines.

With the war going the way that it was, all the Wehrmacht guards were taken away to be used at the front. In their place, we got stuck with civilian SS guards. They were very young and very treacherous. They treated us like the political prisoners they had been obviously toying with, torturing and murdering over at Buchenwald. But by the time we got stuck with the civilian SS guards, we had become a pretty close-knit bunch. We stuck up for the gentiles and they for us. That's just the way it was. We were all victims of the Holocaust. The dark smoke emitted continually by the furnaces at Buchenwald proved it, and we knew it.

But our story has yet to be told, or should I say, has been kept from being told. Our government sure knew about us. We told them. They saw us, they saved us, and shipped us home. But I think that they were frightened that if the American people were to ever hear about what happened to us that they would turn against the Germans as political allies forever, and our government didn't want that. Especially with the Russians sucking up country after country after the war. If Britain and America didn't attempt to befriend somebody, all of Europe would have soon belonged to Russia. So our story was hidden as a result, the atrocities of how Hitler deliberately tried to put us to death, us—American servicemen—the same way he exterminated his political prisoners, by working them to death. And then if that didn't work, I'm sure that they would have considered the gas chamber. Half of us weren't even Jewish. He was just so mad at the time, as were all those that worked under him. It was a crazy time, and somewhere in there we have been forgotten, swept under the rug. But we were as much a part of the damn, terrible Holocaust as any other Jews. But don't tell our government that. No. No way. They wouldn't want our present allies to feel bad about what they and their fathers did and attempted to do to us during the war. As a result of our country's lack of openness, caring, and honesty on their part, we of Berga still suffer with the memory and with the anger that surfaces as the result of no one believing or documenting our story. It hurts. But what hurts even worse is the fact that if we don't learn from what happened the last time, it could happen again.

During our last days in Berga, we were spotted by some of our own reconnaissance planes. They came over the night before our morning evacuation and must have taken photos of the open tunnel and work force on detail. The next day, when we were miles away, the Berga area was devastated. By this time, even our guards had become disgruntled, for they were suffering just like we were. Not nearly as bad as we were, but they were suffering nonetheless. Then one day shortly after we had been spotted, we were marched out of camp as usual. There were only about a hundred of us left by this time. Two hundred of us died in less than two months. But instead of heading off to camp, the guards split us up into two groups of 50 each and marched us in opposite directions. We thought this was going to be the end for us for sure. We thought they were just going to take us out and shoot us, finally be done with us. We kept asking them where we were being taken, but they never answered. Some of the guys started moaning. They thought for sure they were dead. Others started praying, while others begged for their lives. It went on like this for a day or so while we marched until we could see U.S. planes flying over us to Berga and the mines we worked at. Then, and only then, the guards finally decided to tell us what was going on. It appeared that they, too, had taken notice of our reconnaissance planes flying overhead, and they knew that it would only be a short while before our guys, who by that time owned the skies, would be back to close up the mines for good. We were evacuated to be kept from being killed via bombing or strafing. Or I should say that we were evacuated so that they didn't have to stay behind and guard us and get bombed or strafed in the process. For the guards didn't care about us. In fact, at best, they despised us. They only got us out to save their own skins. If it would have been up to them, they would have left us behind to die at the hands of our own pilots while they hightailed it out of there.

At the end, my small group was liberated by the men of the 90th Infantry Division, the other group by the men of the 11th Armored Division. We went on like this, marching and sleeping in some barn for the night, for about three to four days. As you can see, we covered a lot of countryside walking away from each other in the four nights and five days before the Americans came across us, God bless. Until one morning, there was a whole lot of commotion going out in the barnyard outside of the barn we were sleeping in. Then, suddenly, the doors burst open. Again we thought the end was upon us, that the time had finally come. Death had just become such a part of our daily routine that we had become more than familiar with its presence, and had kind of come to expect it. But when the doors burst open, it didn't signal death, but life. For an American infantry regiment had entered the area and were there to free us. Coming out of the barn, I walked right into the barrel of a Sherman tank with one of its big white stars staring right at me. The commander of the tank, a big guy, just picked me right off the ground and put me inside the tank, to give me a lift. He lifted me up by the rope around my overcoat like a kid. He was mad as hell and with his .45 waving in the other hand, begged for me to point him out, the person or person who had done this to me, an American GI. At that moment I did not want any more shooting, I just wanted to be taken away. Finally, the Red Cross showed up with stretchers and everything. But I decided to walk into their nearest hospital.

The next day in a field camp, somewhere in Germany, we were all checked over and then flown in a C-47 to France, where we spent another couple of days in a tent hospital. Then I remember that the war ended and there was a whole lot of commotion. And we were sent to England and put in a modern hospital, where we stayed in bed every minute of the day. Then they began working on fattening us up at the hospital. I went from 90 pounds to 135 pounds. But that didn't necessarily mean that I was healthy. It just meant that I was bigger. They really didn't understand the difference back then, though. In fact, they really didn't know what to do with us. They weren't equipped to handle anything like the problems we brought to them. They'd just never seen anything like us before. The conditions and numbers of POWs for this country was just a whole new thing for everyone. They did the best they could though, even though it was probably only a small fraction of what we really needed.

From England, we were all put aboard a hospital ship and sent on a ten-day cruise across the Atlantic for home. The ship headed for Boston. Then after dropping off some guys there, it took all the guys on board from New York, New Jersey, and Pennsylvania to Staten Island, where we were admitted into another hospital. I stayed in that hospital until about July 4 of that year. Then I was confined to a mental ward for another six months. In January 1946, I was released to Fort Dix, New Jersey, and from there I was released and finally returned home. When we first paraded off the ship in the States, it was a crazy scene. There we were in our PJs, beards and long matted hair walking down the gangplank. Our families were there to greet us. There were big hugs and embraces all around, but we weren't allowed to stay. I just wonder what our families must have thought when they saw us. It must have all been quite a shock. For us, too.

But during those months in the hospitals we all got steadily better. You could see and feel the improvement daily. But the country still didn't know quite what to do with us. Again, large numbers of severely abused POWs was unique to World War II at the time. It was something that had never happened before, without all the automation and long-range bombing and such. So they didn't know how to prepare for us because they didn't know what to expect. So, anyway, they started sending us away on "rest and relaxation" to hotels all over the area, to New York, out to the shore, etc. They'd send us to the theatre, USO clubs, and only the best restaurants. Then they'd bus us back to the hospital. One time we even got to go fishing. It was really nice.

During our stay in the hospital, we kept pretty much to ourselves. We were regimented pretty much to our different theaters of war anyway. There was a lot of guys in from Japan, though. It was nice to see them whenever we did. Their stories were just so different from ours. But then their enemy was just so different as well. Of course, the war wasn't yet over over there either, after I'd returned to the States. So a steady stream of them kept coming in.

But my most memorable recall of my incarceration was our relationship with the unfortunate gentiles that had been singled out with us to be sent to Berga. Though they couldn't understand why they had been chosen, there was never any resentment toward us. In fact, their presence actually helped soothe us. Knowing that they were there and that we weren't all Jewish helped us ease the tensions for ourselves that we were going to be exterminated without ever being given a chance to fight or work for our lives. They were an inspiration, a godsend. Without them and the other prisoners cheering for us at Bad Orb, even more of us would have perished. I just wish they hadn't been forced to go through what we eventually went through. But then I wouldn't wish anything like that on anyone, including our enemies.

John Fellows

John Fellows was one of the non-Jews who were taken to Berga-Elster. Concerning his incarceration, John said: "Faith is definitely an important element in survival, no doubt about it. I think that the basic belief that man is not bad, that element that might come of faith, is really important."

I was captured at the Battle of the Bulge. I guess it was on the 18th or 19th of December. We ended up being corralled with, I would guess, 1,000 other Americans captured. Then we walked about 35 miles back to a town, Gepolsteim or Paum, and were put on trains with a large number of other Americans: people from the division that I was in, the 106th, plus the 28th Division had a large number. We finally unloaded after seven days and nights at Bad Orb near Frankfurt. We arrived sometime around the 27th or 28th of December. We were in barracks 23. There was no question in my recollection that they segregated the Jews when they checked us in by looking at our dog tags, which identified what religion we were. They had C on for Catholic, P for Protestant, H for Hebrew. But we didn't think too much of the fact that they segregated the Jews, although we had heard that Germany was certainly anti-Semitic. But I don't think we had heard anything about the death camps.

So they segregated all the Jews, about 120 men, and they put them in another barracks. There were innumerable barracks at Bad Orb, and in addition to the American units, there were Russians in separate compounds. There were also some other nationalities that they had segregated and put in separate compounds. There were virtually no work details for activities though. The extent of that was that each barracks had someone that would go out and bring back wood for their wood belly stove. That meant a couple of armloads, enough to last an hour or so. I worked on one such detail one time. We went out and cut up some wood right on the Bad Orb grounds. Beyond that, I recall little work. So we never really saw each other. Outside activities consisted of going out to the john, which was just a big outside latrine. So we didn't see too many other people. Then in the afternoon, we would get in line for soup.

When the idea of a separate work detail came up, it did so rather quickly. Our barracks, 23, plus several barracks were named to go. All the Jewish fellas in a separate barracks were to go, and the Germans asked other barracks to furnish their disreputables, which was a guy who was a thief or troublemaker. We didn't really understand what was going on, but we knew something was up. But we weren't really sure who the disreputables were. It wasn't like there was much to steal. Nobody had anything, and most guys were too hungry and weak to be much trouble. We all mostly just kept to ourselves by just trying to keep warm and passing the Bible around. So distinct identification of any disreputables was never made as far as I know, and I was never identified as one. But when we lined up to go the next day, we didn't consider being shipped out to a work camp as such a bad deal, for at least they would have to feed us. We needed food or we weren't going to survive long term.

As far as I can figure, the Germans just wanted 350 people for the work camp we were being sent to. I can't believe, and I have no reason to believe, that the people at Bad Orb knew what we were being sent to Berga for. All I believe the Germans at Bad Orb understood was that we were being shipped off to a work detail. I don't think they thought it was an effort to exterminate us.

We didn't really see very much in the way of German guards or Gestapo at Bad Orb. We went down and were loaded on the boxcars, pretty much at random, just about the same way they had loaded us to take us to Bad Orb. It was a four-day trip, and when we arrived, we knew we were at Berga near Leipzig because we had begun to pick up little pieces of information. We were in a barracks that was pretty new compared to the facilities that we were in at Bad Orb. We were even issued cotton blankets.

We were then divided into two groups, pretty much at random. There was no segregation whatsoever of Jews at any time. So if they stuck together, I wasn't aware of it, and I heard no discussion about it. The group that I was in was the second group to go to work. Now the first group went to work almost the day we got there, and worked two shifts. The first group went off to work in the neighborhood of 10:00 P.M. Then we worked overlapping shifts, something like eight hours and 45 minutes each. I was on the group that went to work about 6:00 or 6:30 in the morning. We were finished around 2:00 or 2:30 P.M. When the first group returned from their first day of work, we were very anxious to know what kind of work they were doing.

They said, "Well, we went in these big holes in the side of this hill and were excavating and shoveling with a pick and shovel, and it is tough."

After we heard how rough the work was, we knew that what we had gotten ourselves into wasn't such a good deal. Our group then went on our first day at 6:00 or 6:30 in the morning and had a pretty good walk from our barracks. The guards had a few German shepherds. We walked to work by the light of carbide lanterns carried by a few in the column of 120 or 150 of us.

After only a few days we got the message that a guy or a couple of guys wanted to make a break for it on the way to our work site. What we did so they could get away was just put all our lights out at the same time, so it would get pitch black. Then they took off. They got away from the group and just kept going. The Germans did a lot of screaming at us, for knocking those carbide flames out and so forth, but nothing else happened. The guys that tried to escape were captured the same day.

But we never discussed anything about being sent away to a camp for Jews and political prisoners. At least, I didn't. I just saw it as what happened to me as a POW. And we really didn't even know that we were in with political prisoners or considered ourselves to be in a segregated camp for Jews. We didn't get much of a chance to talk with any of the other prisoners on the other details, and the Germans didn't seem to treat the Jews any differently than us. Like I said, the dialogue with the other prisoners was at a minimum. There was some trading and all. In fact, I traded a gold signet ring to a Hungarian or Czech, political prisoners working the third shift, for a sandwich, but that was about it.

But in comparison, the conditions were actually better than Bad Orb, cleaner and newer, with the exception that we burned so many more calories on the work details at Berga and had no added food, which was one-fifth or one-sixth of a loaf of bread plus one bowl of soup per day.

In the early going, one guy got jaundice and they took him to the hospital. But I don't remember anybody else being hospitalized in the early going. Though, later on, I remember people that became so ill that they had to be removed from the barracks and were moved into small rooms where they were just left to die, and no attempt was made to stop them from expiring. Now that was after we had been there for a month or so. Then the dying accelerated to the rate of few a day, before it eventually rose to much higher than that, like six or seven per day.

I stayed alive because I was in good physical shape when I was captured, and I was just lucky. I had just turned 19 in September. But if you were to contract virtually any kind of malady, even a common cold, you were so perilously weakened that it would certainly turn into pneumonia or dysentery.   That seemed to be the biggest problem. Once that started, it added a strain on the system, and that was pretty much the end for you. But even with that, there was no discussion that the Germans were trying to annihilate us at all, and no discussion concerning the fact that our camp was considered part of Buchenwald. I never heard that until I read it in a Fort Myers newspaper article. How accurate that was, I'm not really sure. There is some supporting evidence, but I don't know if there is enough to convince me. There was Gestapo around; they were the ones who carried the swords. I do remember them coming around our work details on a few occasions to check on how we were working.

Our situation wasn't high security. Our guards were home guards for the most part. They were feeble-minded and, in a case or two, they were aged people well into their sixties, maybe more than that. They were not very hostile. In fact, our commandant was about as mean to those guards as he was to us. He would just as quickly pistol whip one of those old guards for not walking along or looking like he was falling or slipping as he would an American prisoner. It was sort of a weird sensation watching this happen.

The POWs that survived were guys that were lucky, in pretty good physical condition, and didn't contract some disabling malady. That is how I made it. I got a little touch of yellow jaundice, and I probably didn't work one day. I was lucky they didn't roust me out. That was their tendency. They would come and get you no matter what. Early at Berga, I had stopped eating the bread for a day or two. But then I realized that even if it didn't taste good, I better eat it. The yellow jaundice kind of neutralized and I was able to hang in there.

Then I got put on another work detail with maybe five other guys and no more than one guard. We went out and cut down trees in the forest not far from Berga. On a couple of days, we took a train to a nearby town near the trees we cut down. To show you how screwed up the Germans were, they rousted German civilians out of the compartments of the train and put us in the compartments. We didn't ride the train back; we walked back. So it couldn't have been very far away. It was a strange kind of string of events. They took just a few of us. But we got another slice of bread out there, and we were out in the fresh air rather than stuck in the tunnel all day. I think that helped a little bit, and the weather was getting a little better too, for it was late March or early April. After the tree foresting, I don't think we ever went back in the hole. Then came Easter, and they packed us off to march us away. The Gestapo was not there during that march as I remember. Had there been Gestapo, some of the guys may have tied us to what was happening in Buchenwald [at Berga] through such guards. I should also mention that while we were there we moved to another location, a barracks that was much closer to where we worked. So that cut down our walk by a considerable amount. It was almost in the village of Berga. They relocated the whole detail.

When we got ready for the march away from Berga, they wanted to delouse us. So after taking us into a close-by building one night, they told us to remove all our clothes. They shaved you if you wanted shaved, and they put coal oil on, kerosene, which would kill the lice bugs. But they took our clothes, and this is the part that I have often wondered about, and they put them in some gas ovens. I don't know why we didn't wonder why they had these gas ovens. It was kind of strange. So then they handed the clothes back out to us. I have good recollection of that because I didn't get my own field jacket back. In fact, I got one back that was a bit smaller than mine, so it wasn't very comfortable. The next day we took off on a march, and we walked to a town where we actually stayed in a jail, which was unusual. The next day we kept going. We went on like this, marching during the day and sleeping in barnyards at night, for two-plus weeks until the day after Roosevelt died. I believe he died on April 14. They informed us that Roosevelt had died, and they were rather happy to tell us that. We watched the B-26 bombing in the distance that afternoon. Then after the bombing, we walked down into the town, and they issued us a ration of bread. We hadn't had anything to eat in quite some time. They had bread in a warehouse. I remember our apprehension of walking into the town after the Americans had bombed it. But we really didn't see any evidence of the bombing. That stuck in my mind. We thought that they either did a lousy job of bombing, or we didn't walk where they dropped the bombs. Because of the length of the march and the small amount of food we got, people were beginning to die at an accelerated rate, and on April 17, my best buddy, Ralph Leavitt, died along with six others.

I visited with his brother a number of times after the war, and I hear from him every year. I probably will go see him again shortly. He lives out in Peoria, Illinois. Ralph died in his sleep that night, after he had been on the sick wagon. Once you were on the sick wagon, you were about a day or two from expiring. So as far as I know, he simply died from starvation, and that particular night there were seven who died. I have been back to Germany, a couple of times. Ralph Leavitt's brother has been back there a couple of times, too, and he actually has some photographs of the record of the grave because we buried him in the church yard. The day we buried him we had a sizable work detail, one guy digging for every corpse. I was lucky to have lived. I know how lucky I was because I had diphtheria while I was in Paris after we got released. I was probably on the way to expiring myself if I hadn't gotten out of that prison camp scene. I consider myself pretty lucky, for it was a scary but valuable experience. My faith helped a lot. I became more religious as a result of the experience. I had a Bible and I spent a fair amount of time with it, reading the Bible. Faith is definitely an important element in survival, no doubt about it. I think the basic belief that man is not bad, that element that might come out of faith, is really important.

I can remember looking at a young German the day the Battle of the Bulge started, and he looked like he was 16 to me, and I had just turned 19. I thought, "He doesn't look any different than any of us." If the individuals shooting at each other in most wars were to have their say, I don't think the wars would have taken place. That is the feeling I had, and I think others may have had it as well. It wasn't that anybody was afraid to do what they were supposed to do. Nobody thought there was a just cause to fight. That's all.

I would say that faith is an important aspect, but this guy, Ralph Leavitt, had as much faith as anybody. But considering physical stamina, for whatever odd reason, if you didn't have any, it could eat you up, no matter how much faith you had. I ran into one of the older guys who was in his thirties in Paris, in the 48th general hospital that I went to. I couldn't believe how much he had aged in just those couple of months, for he looked like a 70-year-old. I don't recall his name now. But I was just astounded to run into him looking so old. I just looked at him. The tragedy that haunted him was amazing.

Appendix A: A Perspective on Former Prisoners of War for the 1990s

Charles A. Stenger

During the four major wars of the twentieth century, approximately 142,000 Americans fell into enemy hands. They invariably faced months and years of brutal, inhumane treatment and starvation. Despite this, some 125,000 survived, were returned to U.S. military control, and subsequently to civilian life. Although it was anticipated that these special veterans would have enduring physical and psychological problems as a consequence of these experiences, there was little definitive planning by either the military services or the Veterans Administration. These POWs simply became an invisible part of the far larger total veteran population. Accustomed by captive experience to passively accept the necessity of living with an array of physical and psychological problems, most POWs adjusted to these circumstances without complaint or demand for additional services.

Public awareness of the extremely adverse conditions under which Americans were being held during the Vietnam War brought renewed attention to this issue. Both the military services and Veterans Administration took fresh looks as past efforts, recognized inadequacies, and sought to do a better job with their newest group of POWs. For the VA, this review process brought to the surface continuing deficiencies in services to the far larger populations of POWs from World War II and Korea.

Congress, too, recognized this fact and, in 1978, directed the VA to carry out an extensive study of residual health and adjustment problems of World War II and Korean POWs. By 1980, the VA completed its detailed and comprehensive report, which was excellent in every respect.

In 1981, Congress responded by enacting PL 97-37. This landmark legislation opened up the VA health-care system to all POWs and added anxiety states to the small list of medical conditions that would automatically be presumed a consequence of the prior captive experience. However, the POW still had to prove most medical problems were a direct consequence of those experiences—a-near-impossible task, since pertinent service medical records were grossly inadequate for such purposes or simply non-existent.

Congress subsequently passed three additional laws: PL 98-223 in 1983, PL 99-576 in 1986, and PL 100-322 in 1988. These laws added depressive neurosis, traumatic arthritis, residuals of frostbite, peptic ulcer disease, peripheral neuropathy, and irritable bowel syndrome to the presumptive list. In doing so, Congress relied on available research, including the National Academy of Sciences longitudinal studies, expert opinion, testimony of former POWs, and the findings of the VA Advisory Committee on Former Prisoners of War. These laws also expanded dental benefits and reduced the minimum period of time of captivity for a POW to be eligible for many benefits. However, surprisingly, and perhaps unintentionally, PL 100-322 lowered the priority of POWs for the VA's health-care services.

The VA's participation in this reevaluation process and subsequent expansion of benefits and services can best be characterized as both extremely good and extremely poor. As an agency, the VA has developed many excellent general policies and directives for POWs as a group. However, in implementing these policies for POWs as individuals, the VA has been highly inconsistent. On the positive side, the VA health-care system has responsibly and responsively initiated many steps to ensure an effective response to the medical and psychological needs of individual POWs. Programs to inform and train health-care professionals have been initiated. As a result, many of these professionals have become not only knowledgeable but also deeply involved in the process of understanding and treating POWs. A comprehensive POW Protocol Examination has been developed to increase the understanding of current medical problems in the light of the individual's captive history. Every POW has been offered the opportunity to take this examination, and more than 20,000 have done so. As might be expected, in a very large health-care system confronted by many demands, not all VA medical centers have been fully responsive, yet a determination to achieve this goal is readily apparent.

In stark contrast, the VA's benefit system responsible for the adjudication of POW claims has stubbornly maintained that, with rare exceptions, it has in the past and present fairly and effectively adjudicated individual POW claims. It has done so in the face of overwhelming evidence to the contrary and on the basis of a data system that, at least for POWs, is so grossly inadequate as to be wholly meaningless. Despite all of the broad policy statements and expansion of the presumptive list, the number of POWs formally service-connected for even one condition has actually decreased.

As evidence of this attitude, which has persisted from 1980 to the present, VA officials responsible for the adjudication of veterans' claims have either actively testified against expansion of the presumptive list or, at best, badly stated such additions were wholly "unnecessary." Such testimony was not found to be credible by Congress, which enacted the legislation over the VA's opposition. VA officials in field stations throughout the United States are well aware of the adverse position of their superiors. As a result, and despite general Central Office policy statements supporting more liberal action, field adjudicators have continued prior adjudication policies, denying numerous POWs benefits fully warranted by their captive experiences. In the process, VA often spends far more dollars resisting a claim than the cost of that claim would be over the remaining years of the individual POWS!

The VA POW Advisory Committee has sought since its inception to independently and objectively assess residual medical problems, identify causal relationships to the captive experience, delineate deficiencies in existing adjudication procedures as they apply to POWs, and make recommendations for change. With rare exceptions, the VA has rejected the committee's findings and has even been openly critical. The VA has repeatedly and categorically rejected the recommendation that epidemiological research findings be accepted as other agencies have done, for example, with respect to the health consequences of smoking. Instead, the VA steadfastly requires that a direct etiological relationship be established by clinical research between each individual medical condition and the captive experience.

While ideally such an approach would be preferred, the VA has never initiated such studies due to not only the cost but also the impossibility of designing a research study that would assess the causal relationship of trauma occurring many years in the past to current medical conditions. The tragic consequence of this policy is that it serves to deny needed benefits to many worthy veterans. It is simply not possible that a definitive study of this type could be carried out during the remaining lifetime of the great majority of the approximately 75,000 POWs still alive. As a substitute, the VA is conducting a "study" using the VA Protocol Examination that makes no attempt to ensure that the data is obtained in a systematic, reliable manner by professionals trained to obtain data in a comparable manner in different facilities. This data will be interesting but cannot meet the rigorous scientific standards the VA has informed the committee must be met. In the process, the VA recently constrained the National Academy of Sciences (NAS) from including in its 1988 update of the longitudinal morbidity study data on current health factors that heretofore have always been included in these reports. Presumably, it will be delayed for an indeterminate period of time to be included in VA's protocol study. Such a delay seems wholly unwarranted and unnecessary since it has independent merit and is clearly needed by a rapidly decreasing POW population. That 1988 report was therefore limited to depressive symptoms. It is important and does confirm that significant degrees of depression are currently present in the POW population and can be linked by compelling evidence to events suffered during the captive experience many years earlier.

There are many areas in which the objective and authoritative assessment by the VA's Advisory Committee on Former Prisoners of War is still badly needed. It is hoped that legislation that established VA as a cabinet-level department will result in a more open, less defensive stance by the VA on adjudication of POW claims. In this respect, it is noted that the VA has agreed to accept epidemiological findings on Vietnam veterans exposed to Agent Orange.

Evidence tying later health problems to POW deprivations is considerably stronger and has the support of almost every expert in this area. The medical representatives on the Advisory Committee had unanimously agreed not only that every body system could be damaged by the hardship of the captive experience, but also that the capacity of the immune system to thwart the development of many medical problems was reduced by those adversities.

We hope that needed services and benefits to remaining POWs will become a reality in the 1990s. As a part of this, the VA should modify its stringent evidentiary requirements for POW claims; give them the benefit of the doubt; seek to restore top priority for eligibility for health-care services, add liver disease to the presumptive list; and take other necessary steps to ensure that POWs are in fact provided the full range of benefits and services they continue to need and have unquestionably earned. As the Advisory Committee noted in previous reports, POWs, despite many health problems, have not imposed unreasonable demands on the VA but, instead, have characteristically waited many years before seeking help from the VA. When they do, they should be treated with compassion and respect fitting for those who sacrificed so much for their country.

Appendix B: Soldiers of Berga

Ray Weiss

HOW THIS STORY CAME TO LIGHT

The story of Berga first came to the attention of *News-Press* staff writer Ray Weiss when he interviewed Bernie Melnick in connection with another story.

Melnick, 59, lives in Cape Coral. He was one of the survivors of Berga, a slave-labor camp where he and 349 other American soldiers, mostly Jews, were imprisoned by Nazi captors during World War II. In February 1983, Melnick agreed to talk about his experiences at the camp, but only after other Jewish survivors verified his story. He didn't want to be accused of making up wild tales about a bunch of GIs being singled out and sent to a concentration camp.

"I don't want to rattle any cages after 38 years, I'm not looking for any glory," he said.

Weiss was able to find five other survivors. Berga wasn't a fictitious tale.

The former POWs were found in California, New York, and Massachusetts, and they gave the same account as Melnick. Melnick said he planned to correspond with the men. But he had one regret.

"By now so many of the boys who survived Berga must be dead," he said. "Probably no more than a handful, maybe 25 to 40 of us are left."

Reprinted from the *News-Press*, Fort Myers, Fla, May 1, 1983, by permission.

Somehow the tragedy of Berga evaded history. No government record exists concerning the few hundred American prisoners of war who spent the last months of World War II in a German slave-labor camp—most because they were Jews—where they were beaten, starved, and worked to death. But Berga happened.

It was early February 1945, and the war in Europe was nearing an end. The once powerful German military was collapsing. Optimism filled the American and Allied ranks as they pushed toward Berlin and victory.

But inside Berga, a German slave-labor camp on the Elster River near the Czech border, about 350 American prisoners of war fought individual battles of survival. Along with the Jewish soldiers were other GIs who were considered undesirable by the Nazis for one reason or another. The Americans worked alongside religious and political prisoners from Eastern European countries, such as Poland and Hungary.

Treatment at the camp bordered on genocide. Only 90 to 125 Americans are estimated to have survived the three-month ordeal. No survivor weighed more than 90 pounds when liberated. The story of these World War II veterans has gone untold through the years. The survivors provide the only proof the incident occurred. The Germans destroyed most concentration and slave-labor camp documents before the end of the war. The United States military and government historians do not have any knowledge that Jewish-American POWs ever were singled out and persecuted by the Germans.

"I have never heard of American soldiers being segregated and treated like this," said George Wagner, a federal employee dealing with captured German records. "I don't know what activity took place in that camp, because we don't have those records. After December 1944, the Germans destroyed most."

Alfred Feldman, a survivor of Berga, said he gave a deposition about his ordeal to military war-crimes investigators after the war. But what happened to that information is a mystery to Feldman and the United States military archives department. The agency, as well as all others dealing with military matters, has no information about American POWs being in Berga. Feldman is upset by what he perceives as disinterest by the United States military.

"It makes me bitter. Our government buried the whole thing. Our depositions were never used against our captors. Why, I don't know. I guess we were just a very small group of men, a few hundred fellas who got lost in the shuffle and confusion," Feldman said. "No one cared then what happened to us. It was the end of the war."

What happened in Berga is believed to have been an isolated incident of German brutality against American prisoners. In other German POW camps, Jewish-Americans at times were segregated from fellow soldiers and housed in separate barracks. But none is believed to have been mistreated on the scale of what happened in Berga.

Why the Germans singled out this group of men is unknown. Opinions differ among the survivors. Some say it was a directive from Hitler that Jewish POWs be removed from all camps, but that only the Berga camp commander carried out the order. Others say it was an individual decision by an anti-Semitic camp commander in Berga. Whatever the reason, many of the men who survived the slave-labor camp continue to live with the horror and pain they witnessed and endured. They cannot escape the memories.

Bernie Melnick was just a few days past his twenty-first birthday when he fell in for roll call on that cold February morning with the rest of the prisoners at Bad Orb Stalag 9B. The young private first class had been at the POW holding facility east of Frankfurt since his capture a month earlier at the Battle of the Bulge—Hitler's last major counterattack. The overcrowded camp held prisoners from many Allied countries.

Life was cramped, but the food, shelter, and treatment provided by the Germans were satisfactory. The men even received letters and packages from home. Within a day, all that would change.

Melnick and the other prisoners listened as an order was read that all Jews would be transferred to a place called Berga the next morning. The soldiers were told to report to a separate barracks, where they would await the move.

"The Yanks were crossing the Rhine, and the Krauts wanted to get rid of any possible troublemakers. They were afraid the Jews might revolt," the 59-year-old Cape Coral retiree recalled. "All day I pondered what to do. Would I be a Jew or wouldn't I? By nightfall I decided I was. I reported to the barracks."

Jewish and non-Jewish soldiers argued with their captors about the illegality of the action. Talk was futile, however. Non-Jewish prisoners encouraged their Jewish counterparts to lie about their religion. Some did, throwing away identification tags. A few escaped into areas of the camp where British, French, and Russian prisoners were housed. But most maintained their religious identity and checked into the barracks.

Private Ernest Kinoy wrestled with his conscience. When he was captured at the Battle of the Bulge, Kinoy threw away his dog tags, not wanting to reveal his religion. He told the Germans he was Protestant. But that night, he too decided to join the other Jewish soldiers.

"I didn't want to make it easy for the Germans. But they usually got the information they wanted," Kinoy, a New York City scriptwriter, recalled. "When they didn't, they just had men stand out in the snow until they told. Someone would have eventually informed them I was Jewish."

Kinoy wrote a television play in the early 1950s about his prison camp experiences. That script is believed to be all that ever has been published about the men sent to Berga. But Sybil Milton, an expert in German-Jewish history, is familiar with stories about the POWs in Berga.

"No one has done research on this. There's not one book you can turn to. It's my feeling it's true, that it happened. I've met people who said this happened to them," the New York City historian said.

The national archives department has a record of the men leaving Bad Orb on February 8, 1945, destination unknown. But the men who survived Berga do not need official confirmation of where they were sent. They know what they experienced.

The Germans at Bad Orb wanted to send only Jewish POWs to Berga. It's estimated that between 150 and 200 were identified and moved to the slave-labor camp. But the Germans needed 350 men to meet their quota. Some of the "undesirable" non-Jews chosen were considered thieves and troublemakers by the Germans. Others were picked at random because they had stereotypical Jewish looks or names. And still others were selected just because they were circumcised, something the German soldiers thought might be the mark of a Jew.

Norman Fellman, a Berga survivor, remembered that one anti-Semitic American he knew—a Christian soldier with the last name of Zion—was picked.

"He kept denying he was Jewish. But they didn't listen," the New York City shoe store owner said. "He died just before we were liberated. It's quite ironic."

The POWs were scared the morning they left Bad Orb. The German guards assured them everything would be fine, that they were being sent to a quiet place, a farm or factory. But stories had circulated by then about Jews being exterminated in concentration camps. The men worried that the same fate awaited them.

Sporadic violence flared as many Jewish and non-Jewish POWs objected to the move. The guards retaliated, pushing the men back into the ranks. When order was restored, the Americans were marched out of camp and down a hill into town. Within a couple of hours, they were packed into boxcars like cattle and shipped across the German countryside to Berga.

About 60 men shared each compartment during the weeklong trip. The only food the men ate was what they packed on themselves. Their bed was a floor filled with straw. Their toilet was a single bucket. Within a couple of days, the car reeked from the smell of human waste. No sunlight and little air filtered through the car. The men tried to keep their spirits up, but fear and uncertainty kept them down.

During the trip, the train was strafed and bombed by Allied aircraft. The boxcar ahead of Melnick's was hit. He helped bury the dead.

"We didn't know who they were—if they were guys like us or if they were civilian Jews. We spent two hours in the dark digging a trench for the bodies. Then we got back on the train."

Several days later, the train pulled into Berga. The American soldiers were unloaded and marched about 40 miles from town to the work camp.

Conditions were much worse in Berga than in Bad Orb. The barracks consisted of about 30 bunk beds, with mattresses of burlap bags filled with straw. A single pot-bellied charcoal stove provided the only heat inside each shack. No blankets or winter clothing were issued to protect men from the below-freezing weather. Many still wore only the tattered uniforms in which they were captured. The one main meal each day consisted of a bowl of hot water with a few undefinable objects floating on top. When they were lucky, the men received a piece of bread the size of a half dollar. Most days, they were unlucky.

The American POWs worked seven days a week from sunrise to sunset, boring rock out of the middle of a mountain. Other crews, mainly civilian prisoners, worked at night.

The Americans rarely talked with the civilians, who wore striped clothing and skull caps. There usually was little to say, as each prisoner isolated himself, trying to block out the death and disease around him.

It's believed the Germans were rushing to build a V-2 plant in Berga. The missiles became a popular weapon for the Nazis toward the end of the war.

As the days passed, the men grew weaker. Their weight plummeted and their resistance to disease waned. At least one American died each day. Yet few men tried to escape. Most could muster just enough energy to walk.

"Toward the end, we were walking zombies," Melnick said. "Once four guys tried to escape, and they were caught and shot through the head. The Krauts brought them back to the camp and left them to show us what would happen if others tried.

"We Jewish boys stayed together. We didn't try to break out. We didn't want to give the Krauts any excuse to treat us worse. As it was, we were being persecuted."

The survivors recall no Americans being exterminated. But sometimes screams could be heard at night from the other side of the complex, where the civilian Jews were housed.

"I later found out the Germans had skinned people alive there," Feldman said. "They were afraid to do anything like that to us. They knew the war was lost and didn't want the Americans to retaliate."

However, life for civilian Jewish prisoners was quite different. The Germans did not fear retaliation from them.

Berga was a satellite camp of Buchenwald, a major concentration camp to the northwest, near Weimar. Most of the civilian prisoners had spent time at Buchenwald and witnessed countless atrocities.

"We only saw the civilians when we changed shifts. But sometimes, as we passed them, they told us what was going on. They told us that the Germans were killing Jews by any means," Feldman said.

During the final weeks at Berga, more and more POWs died of starvation and pneumonia. Bodies were stacked as many as four-high against the fence that surrounded the compound. No body would be buried until a doctor signed a prisoner's death certificate. It was a rule.

The doctor visited the camp just once every couple of weeks. His job dealt more with the dead than with the living. Few prisoners received any medical attention.

Kinoy was an exception. He fell off a scaffold and hurt his back badly a month after he arrived at Berga. A doctor transferred Kinoy to a German hospital, where he remained until the end of the war.

In a way, the death of a POW provided a strange benefit for the others. With luck, a man was selected for a burial squad, missing a few hours of blasting and loading rock out of the mountain.

Their former colleague was placed on a cart and pushed by the men into town, where a casket-maker quickly assembled a makeshift wooden coffin. While in town, the POWs could beg for food scraps and cigarette butts from the local residents. Then they buried their former companion outside a civilian cemetery, taking with them any piece of clothing they could use. In Berga, dignity existed only in death. The men had to compromise their values in the hope of surviving another day.

Life was a constant struggle. But Jewish survivors, such as Melnick, Kinoy, Feldman, and Fellman, said the Germans made no distinction between the POWs because of religion.

"We all got terrible treatment, not just the Jews. No food. No medicine. Everyone was sick and filled with lice," Feldman said. "We were beaten on the job for any excuse. They'd hit us all with a rifle butt just for the hell of it."

But Joseph Guigno, an Italian-American POW, disagreed. No Jewish soldiers lived in his barracks, but he heard stories about their mistreatment. "The Germans would push the sick ones around. We heard about one Jew with pneumonia who was dragged out of bed one morning. The Germans threw a bucket of cold water on him, and he died.

"All of us were treated like animals. But the Jewish boys got the worst. They were beaten more and given less food."

The men tried not to dwell on their dilemma, though. As they laid in their bunks at night, they could hear the Allied bombs and shells exploding in the distance. Each night the sound grew louder, closer. The POWs knew the war was ending.

All now suffered from dysentery, malnutrition, and combinations of infected wounds and disease. Some could no longer walk. Living came down to each man's strength of spirit.

"I remember all I thought about all the time was surviving. In the end, that's what separated those who did from those who didn't," Guigno said.

In early April 1945, the men lined up outside the barracks for the usual trek to the mountain. But this time, the German guards marched the prisoners in the opposite direction. They left in stages. The final days were becoming what the survivors call "the death march."

Initially, the Americans believed they were being relocated to another camp. But for nearly three weeks, the Germans marched the prisoners aimlessly along country roads, trying to avoid the liberating American and Russian forces as long as possible.

Those who couldn't walk were placed in carts. Food was scarce and, at night, the men slept in barns and abandoned buildings. "Guys were dying like flies," Melnick said.

A few miles up the road, the civilian prisoners, an estimated 20,000, led the way. Old World War I veterans guarded the Americans, while the Nazi SS handled the civilian prisoners. The civilians who lagged behind the pack were murdered and left beside the road.

Feldman remembers the scene. "The SS couldn't shoot them fast enough. The only thing that saved us was we weren't guarded by the SS."

Americans received special treatment from the old soldiers. In fact, the last couple of days, the guards became friendlier, hoping for kind treatment in return when they became prisoners. One old soldier saved Feldman's life, when the POW was mistaken for a civilian by a member of the SS.

Feldman fell on the road, and when he looked up, a pistol was pointing down at his face. "I thought I was dead. But one of the old guards pulled the SS guy away and told him I was a POW."

The ordeal finally ended in late April for the men of Berga. Melnick's liberation day was April 28th. Today it means as much to him as a birthday or an anniversary. Thirty-eight years have passed, and the memory of that spring morning remains clear.

The prisoners sharing a country barn sensed something different was happening as they awoke for another day on the road. They heard no German voices, only shooting outside. One POW climbed a ladder and looked out from a window to investigate.

"I see a big white star! It looks like a Sherman tank!" he hollered down to his companions. The men cheered. It was American.

"Before we knew it the barn door flew open and it wasn't a Kraut standing there. They were hiding by then," Melnick recalled, as his voice filled with emotion. "I ran over to some tank and the commander picked me up and lifted me inside. I was hysterical. Between that and having dysentery, I was all over the place."

Melnick weighed 90 pounds when liberated. Besides dysentery, he also suffered from jaundice, infected wounds, and shell shock.

Nine days later, Germany surrendered. By then, Melnick and the other survivors were recuperating in English or French hospitals. Most would not see each other again, as they found their niche in life. But they always would share a common bond—the nightmare of Berga.

"I've never forgotten the place. What happened to us there was so unbelievable, we didn't believe it ourselves," Feldman said. "It wasn't supposed to happen to American boys. But it did."

Appendix C: Christmas Story

Mario Garbin

The view through the narrow crack in the side of the tiny German boxcar was breathtaking. A soft white blanket of snow had covered the ground during the night and somehow it brought back to me with sharp poignancy the memory of other lovely days in happier circumstances. Young fir trees poked their heads out of the snow, the upper limbs looking for all the world like shoulders with epaulets of white. They stood at attention, row upon row, stretching as far as the eye could see. The setting was too peaceful to inspire thoughts of things military. Funny, though, the things that run through your mind looking at a scene so familiar and yet so different from the ones at home.

The lines, "Two men stood looking through prison bars, one saw mud, the other stars," kept running through my mind like some of the goofy ditties that were sung as commercials over the radio at home. How long ago was that? It was years and years ago, so long ago that memories oftentimes blurred and assumed unreality. You know what I mean. It's happened to you, too. You think of some tragic thing that happened to you in the past and in thinking of it you wonder if you didn't dream the whole thing and that soon you'll awaken and find a flood of relief surging through your body. And yet it was only four days ago that we were taken in the Ardennes forest just inside Germany. A lifetime of hopelessness and misery and despair crammed into four days.

They had marched us for three days to Gerolstein, where some 1,500 of us were jammed 70 to a car, most of which reeked of horse urine and manure. We had left the town the night before and had traveled approximately six kilometers when we had bumped to a stop and spent the rest of the night there.

This morning was the day before Christmas. It was bitterly cold, with a dry penetrating sharpness that made sitting for more than half an hour pure torture. Whatever heat our bodies provided was sucked away by the cold air that swept through the car. I moved away from my vantage point dispiritedly and took a position on the floor. It was dark in the car, the only light coming from the one window set high up in one corner. My thoughts were a potpourri of everything I had ever done, spiced with real fear of what the future held in store for me as a prisoner of war. I was out of smokes, and asking any of the men for one was out of the question. In just a few days, we had already developed a selfishness indicative of the fear of want that was to torture us in the future.

I knew only one man in that car, Trex Trexler. We had been assigned to the 106th Infantry at about the same time. Trex was a veteran of the Aleutian campaign and was a sort of battalion VIP because of his having held the lightweight boxing championship of the Aleutian area. Trex sat on my right, and on my left was a southern boy. His name was Bolling—a cook with one of the outfits on the 106th right flank. I introduced myself to another GI. Siebert, his name was, and I think he said he was a heavy weapons specialist. Siebert, I found, came from Pittsburgh, Pennsylvania, my home town, and we talked a little bit about things that GIs from the same hometown usually talk about. We made the usual GI promises to look up each other after the war and have several drinks to our European memories.

While talking with Siebert, I popped a Life Saver into my mouth and Siebert asked if I wanted to trade. I had perhaps half a package, and I swapped it for a package of Half and Half pipe tobacco. Just as we had completed the transaction, one of the men took a Bible from his pocket and suggested that I read aloud the journey into Bethlehem. I was too confused, too full of the thoughts of all my loved ones. I was afraid that I would break down while reading, so I refused.

Siebert volunteered. The only light in the car was directly opposite me and just touching Siebert's shoulder. His voice trembling in spots, he recreated for us the sufferings of Mary and Joseph in their search for shelter. I was awfully quiet. The awareness of the necessity for prayer was heavy in the car and you knew that the men were thinking the same thoughts as you. Despite our condition, we were still damned lucky to be alive, and it was about time we thanked God for his goodness to us. As Siebert finished reading, we heard the drone of planes.

Like puppets responding to the manipulator, all heads turned toward the GI standing at the window. He shrugged his shoulders and then, taking a second look, yelled, "Spitfires!" We sat motionless, soundless. They passed overhead and we began to breathe a little more freely. Then came that crescendo of sound made by planes peeling off from formation, preparatory to an attack. The sound leaves you like a wrung-out dishrag.

After the first frenzied scurrying for cover, the only thing that seems alive is that heart of yours pounding furiously, sending the blood in fast pulsations to your ears as if seeking escape from your body.

We hit the floor, men fighting for the best positions, as if any of them were good. Our car was sixth from the engine and, as we heard the first bursts of the .50-calibre bullets and the powerful sound of the bursting 20mm shells also used by the Spitfires, I could see in my mind's eye the bursts stitching a deadly pattern in the floor.

The Tommies strafed that train from engine to caboose and, since the guards had locked the doors the night before, we had to take that gunning like sitting birds, and from our own guys, too. Finally, someone managed to break open the doors and we piled out into the snow to form a huge "POW USA." The planes had started back for another run when they noticed the letters in the snow and they waggled their wings in acknowledgment and left.

While we were milling around after the planes left, my right foot began to hurt unbearably and I bent to examine it. It looked funny to me. I never knew I had such a small foot. I removed the boot and saw that it was a size 8½. One of the phenomena of war, I thought. Here I am, a 200-pounder wearing a size 11. And in the confusion immediately before leaving the cars, I had reached out blindly for my shoes and managed to squeeze my foot into the comparatively petite size 8½. I finally found the owner and regained my original footwear.

The left side of my coat was soaked with blood. Then I remembered that Bolling had dived between me and Trex and that one of the 20mm shells had gotten him in the arm. The last thing I remember was his monotonous repetition of the words: "Let me out, I'm bleeding to death." We checked on the occupants of our car and found that Bolling had been the only one hit. God was good to us, we said.

We suddenly became aware that this was the first clear day in the last week and a half. As near as I can recall, a heavy fog had settled over all that part of Germany the 14th and 15th of December 1944, and the fog had persisted up to December 24.

Then we heard the sound of a great many planes in the distance. The horizon was almost literally darkened by bombers coming from England and France. I guess every man in that group began to yell with joy to see our planes finally in the air to give the Allies the support we had needed so desperately with the start of the Battle of the Bulge on December 16. There were B24s, Mosquito bombers, and Lancasters coming in wave after wave. The American planes were not camouflaged—a bright aluminum shining in the sun.

And then, not more than 300 yards from us, a German anti-aircraft gun opened up on the planes. It was a sound I had never heard before, obviously a heavy calibre, and it shot in a sequence of two, with a couple of seconds in between each shot. I think out of the first six rounds, that gun hit five of our planes, two of which plunged crazily to the earth. One other began to veer off, obviously trying to make a turn to return to Allied territory. The fourth disintegrated in the air in one ball of flame, and the fifth broke in half. The tail section kind of lazily floated down, and the forward section with the wings began to spiral flatly to earth. I know I prayed, and I suppose everybody else did, to see parachutes. On figure hurtled from the tail section and a chute opened. Four others blossomed out of the forward section. I could hear the man next to me saying, "Come on, three more." But that's all that came out. For some reason, the anti-aircraft gun fired no more.

And then we felt the earth begin to tremble as the planes that had passed over a half hour before obviously were bombing their targets. That bombing went on for hours. I could imagine the carnage that must have been the lot of German cities that day.

As it began to get dark, we decided that it was safe enough to return to the cars. As we started back into the doors, no one spoke, no one looked at the ripped sides and roof, and our joy at being delivered was stilled. We had forgotten one man. On the seat was a body, torso erect, head back, stomach and entrails in its lap. It was Siebert, Bible in hand, finger marking the passage: "Peace on earth."

Appendix D: American Victims of the Holocaust

Mitchell G. Bard

Switching channels on my television set not long ago, I ran across "P.O.W.—Americans in Enemy Hands," a documentary on American prisoners of war. In it, one World War II veteran gave a startling account of how he and his fellow Jewish prisoners had been segregated from their comrades in a prisoner-of-war camp and sent to a slave-labor camp. There, Jewish prisoners of war were beaten, starved, and literally worked to death.

This was the first I had ever heard of American victims of the Holocaust, and it stimulated me to investigate whether there indeed had been American Jews among the six million exterminated by the Nazis. I contacted Holocaust research institutes, survivors' organizations, military archives, and veterans' groups and discovered that there are only a few oblique references to American Jews who might have been killed as part of the "final solution." Rather than indicating that no American Jews died at the hands of the Nazis, the lack of information reflects the sad fact that these victims' stories have gone untold.

Remarkably, there is virtually no mention of Americans in any of the major or even minor works concerning the Holocaust. One of the few references appears in Martin Gilbert's *Atlas of the Holocaust*, which lists 17 American natives who were deported to Auschwitz, ten of whom he says were U.S. citizens. Apparently, none survived. One American who did live to tell about his experience in a concentration camp was Barry Spanjaard. His book, *Don't Fence Me In*, documents that nightmare.

Reprinted from *The Jewish Veteran*, Fall 1990, by permission.

Spanjaard was born in America, but his parents were Dutch and had taken him back to Holland. In 1940, at the age of ten, he had been advised by the American consul to return to the United States but was told he would have to go without his parents. He refused. Three years later, after the Nazis had overrun Holland, his family was deported to a transit camp at Westerbork, 30 miles from the German border. During their time in the camp, two American fliers who had been shot down were brought in, but Spanjaard never learned what happened to them.

On January 31, 1944, the 14-year-old youth was put on a train with his parents to Bergen-Belsen, where he spent the next year. On January 21, 1945, while his father was in the hospital, he and his mother were called into the commandant's office and asked whether they wanted to go to the United States. Although skeptical, they accepted the offer. Spanjaard then carried his 39-year-old father, who weighed only 65 pounds, past the gate to a truck, starting their journey to the Swiss border. Spanjaard's father had survived for two years in concentration camps, but he died after just three days of freedom.

Spanjaard learned later that the Germans had decided to trade him to the Americans for five German POWs. He now says that the Germans had wanted to make a trade for him from the beginning, but the U.S. government had refused. Eight years later, during the Korean War, Spanjaard was sent back to Germany by the U.S. Army. "If I had known then that the American government had done nothing to save me," he bitterly says today, "I would never have fought for this country."

There are a few other references to Americans being in concentration camps. Olga Lengyel's book about Auschwitz, *Five Chimneys*, for example, quotes Dr. Albert Wenger, an American lawyer and economist who was in Vienna when Hitler declared war. Wenger said he was arrested on February 24, 1943, by the Gestapo for sheltering a Jewish woman and was deported to Auschwitz. Wenger said that while he was at Auschwitz, he heard that an American named Herbert Kohn was gassed in January 1944. Another American, known only as Myers, was also gassed, according to Wenger. He said he could cite other cases but could not remember the victim's names.

In his book *Dachau* (1975), Paul Berben cites a Polish source who said there were 11 Americans in that death camp on April 26, 1945, but that no Americans died, according to the death certificates. The Office for Strategic Services (OSS, the wartime forerunner for the Central Intelligence Agency) reported finding six Americans among the 31,432 prisoners liberated from Dachau. According to a *New York Times* account on May 1, 1945, one U.S. major caught behind the lines on a mission for the OSS was among those liberated. In May 1945, about the time Mauthausen was liberated, there were eight Americans reported there, four of whom were Jews, according to Evelyn Le Chene, in her book, *Mauthausen*.

There were approximately 600,000 Jews in the U.S. armed services. According to Lt. Col. Martin Goller, who wrote "American Jews in World War II" (published in 1984 in Issac Kowaslki's *Anthology on Armed Jewish Resistance 1939–1945: vol. 1*), 8,000 Jews were killed in action, 2,500 died in service, and over 18,000 were wounded in combat. These soldiers were casualties of war, but there were others among those who were captured who became victims of the Holocaust.

For the generation that grew up watching "Hogan's Heroes" on television, it is easy to have gotten the impression that POW camps in Germany were relatively benign places run by bumbling Nazis. The truth was that while German POW camps were nothing like the concentration and death camps, they were very harsh places where thousands of American soldiers died. In fact, according to A. J. Barker, in *Behind Barbed Wire*, the death toll for prisoners during World War II reached an unprecedented level, estimated at between 6 million and 10 million. Approximately 11 percent of all British and American prisoners and 60 percent of the Russian prisoners died in captivity, most from malnutrition and neglect. Although there appear to have been few cases of persecution of Jewish soldiers, Jewish POWs I interviewed were frightened throughout their imprisonment and were constantly aware of the possibility that they could be sent to a concentration camp.

These fears were a result of knowledge not only of what was happening to Jewish civilians, but also of what had happened to other POWs, notably Soviet Jewish prisoners. In 1941, Hitler issued the Commissar Order, which called for the elimination of political representatives and commissars, whom he considered the "driving forces of Bolshevism." Included in the extermination order were all Soviet Jews. In July 1941, all Jewish POWs from the eastern front were ordered to be killed. No similar order was ever made concerning Jewish POWs from Britain, France, or the United States. The reason may be that despite Nazi propaganda that the Allies did not care about Jews, the Germans thought those nations would care very much if Jews from their armies became victims. A more likely explanation was that the Nazis were concerned that German POWs would be mistreated if the Western nations learned that Jewish prisoners were being abused. But the apparent failure of the United States to investigate mistreatments of Jewish POWs implies that Nazi propaganda was correct: The United States did not even care about its own Jews.

One POW camp where the possibility of deportation to a concentration camp nearly became a reality was Stalag Luft 1 in the town of Barth, near the Black Sea. After the bombing of Dresden in 1945, Jews in the camp were segregated by the Nazis with the collaboration of the American prison-block captain. Some Jews threw away their dog tags or tried to hide their identity, but the Germans had their own methods of distinguishing prisoners. According to John Vietor, a former prisoner who wrote of his wartime experiences in *Time Out*,

The goons posted a list of names in each barracks, supposedly the names of the Jewish officers concerned. Vaunted German thoroughness was noticeably lacking in the capricious manner in which they had decided who was Jewish and who wasn't. Kellys and O'Briens were included and a few Cohens left out, much to the bafflement and concern of the kriegies [prisoners] involved.

Another former prisoner of Luft 1, Sam Kalman, explained that the block captain used the excuse that the 120 Jewish officers were to be sent to a "central" camp, but there was little doubt in the minds of the prisoners that this meant a concentration camp. Kalman, who described his experience in his article, "An Ex-P.O.W. Remembers" (the *Jewish Veteran*, July-August 1986), believes that had the Germans won the Battle of the Bulge, the deportation order would have been carried out.

While in the camp, the Jews were not mistreated. In fact, another former prisoner, Ed Neft, told me that they were permitted to conduct religious services, which they did at least partially "to piss the Nazis off." For his book on American POWs, *For You the War Is Over*, David Foy spoke to former prisoners from a number of POW camps, and each confirmed that, for the most part, Jewish prisoners were not treated differently from others.

One former prisoner told Foy that the Germans at Luft 3 had deep prejudices against Jews and permitted the guards to try to incite other POWs against the Jews, but the prisoners remained united and kept the number of Jews a secret from the Germans. Foy also learned of a few cases in which American Jewish POWs were victims of "special treatment" that ranged from various types of discrimination to physical abuse. At Luft 3, for example, the Germans relieved the cook of his duties after they discovered he was Jewish. At 2B, the Germans refused to negotiate with Private Harry Goller, the so-called "man of confidence" (MOC) elected by his comrades to represent them to the commandant, when they learned he was Jewish. They had dealt with him for nearly a year before that. In Stalag 9B, east of Frankfurt, the MOC refused to segregate Jewish prisoners; the Germans did so themselves according to their perception of who they thought was Jewish. According to an intelligence report prepared by the War Department in November 1945, Jewish POWs in Stalag 7A, in Bavaria, 22 miles northeast of Munich, were also segregated but not otherwise mistreated. Foy noted that the worst persecution some Jewish POWs endured was from fellow prisoners who sometimes verbally abused them.

The Red Cross also reported that there was no inequality in the treatment of Jewish prisoners. The organization did acknowledge that Jewish

POWs were sometimes segregated but accepted the Nazi contention that such actions were permissible under Article 9 of the Geneva Convention, which provides that belligerents shall not house prisoners of different races or nationalities together. In Luft 1, Ed Neft said, the Nazis had convinced the American barracks leader to go along with a separation of British and American POWs under this provision despite protests by junior officers, who presciently warned that allowing such segregation would set a bad precedent. When Jews were ordered segregated, the Germans argued that it was just another separation of races and nationalities.

Evidence of American soldiers sent to concentration camps is limited. For example, in *Beyond the Last Path*, Eugene Weinstock explains that by March 1945, Buchenwald had become "the last and final stop for all imprisoned anti-fascist Europe." The Nazis planned to destroy the camp so that no evidence of the atrocities committed there would remain. Before the destruction of the camp, however, the prisoners were to be killed. "Only American and British war prisoners could hope for life since they were under the jurisdiction of the regular German army rather than the SS murderers," Weinstock wrote.

The presence of American POWs in concentration camps was disputed, however, by a congressional committee that visited Buchenwald, Nordhausen, and Dachau in April 1945 at the request of General Eisenhower and submitted a detailed report of the shocking conditions they found in the camps.

"In the first place," the report stated, "the concentration camps for political prisoners must not be confused with prisoner of war camps. No prisoners of war are confined in any of these political-prisoner camps, and there is no relationship whatever between a concentration camp for political prisoners and a camp for prisoners of war."

There were indeed distinctions between the types of camps, but many POWs were sent to concentration camps—including those visited by the committee—where the prisoners were tortured and killed. Most of those sent to the concentration camps were Poles and Russians, so perhaps they were of less concern to the Americans. But according to Paul Foreman, in an article in May 1959 in *Social Forces*, there had also been a few British and American POWs in Buchenwald before the delegation arrived. In addition, repatriation reports written by prisoners who had been in German camps reveal that there had been about 30 American POWs in Buchenwald.

Evidence was also presented at the Nuremberg trials of the mistreatment of Allied soldiers. A report by the U.S. Third Army's investigating officer cites cases of murder, "by shooting, beating, use of poison gas, drowning, starvation, injections, stoning, exposure, burning, and choking of nationals of 23 nations, including members of the U.S. armed forces."

There were numerous atrocities committed against soldiers, particularly at Mauthausen. Two former prisoners testified at Nuremberg about the presence and killing of Americans, but there was no mention of whether or not they were Jews. Lt. Jack Taylor was sent to Mauthausen after being captured in Austria. He testified that conditions in the camp amounted to a sentence of death by starvation and torture and that at least two American officers were killed in the gas chambers. Taylor and another American officer were also to be killed but were saved by the advancing U.S. Army, which liberated the camp.

The one clear example of American Jewish soldiers becoming victims of the Holocaust occurred in Berga, a little-known subcamp of Buchenwald. Daniel Steckler had been in Luxembourg in December 1944, when he was captured by the Germans.

"The most fearful thing to me was the fact that, as a Jew, I carried a dog tag that had a great big 'H' on it, standing for Hebrew," he said in the documentary, "P.O.W.," "and I didn't think that I would last for five minutes."

When the Germans were not looking, Steckler ripped off his tag and threw it in the snow. "It made me feel goddamned mad," he recalled bitterly, "because it made me feel as though I was tearing a piece of me off." He was then put in a cattle car for seven days with over 60 other people and no food.

Soon after Steckler arrived at the POW camp, 4,000 American prisoners were assembled in a field while the commandant ordered all Jews to take one step forward. Word ran through the ranks not to move. The non-Jews told their Jewish comrades that they would stand with them. The commandant then said they would have until 6:00 the next morning to identify themselves. The prisoners were told, moreover, that any Jews in the barracks after 24 hours would be shot, as would anyone trying to hide or protect them. The American in charge of the prisoners' barracks filed a Red Cross protest, which the Nazis ignored.

Bernie Melnick, then a 21-year-old private who had been captured in the Battle of the Bulge, debated whether to admit that he was a Jew. The non-Jews encouraged their comrades to deny they were Jewish, and some did, but Melnick decided not to hide his identity.

Steckler faced the same dilemma: "Was I to be told to lower myself into a sewer, to deny myself, to deny who and what I was? Never. You may kill me, but you'll never destroy me."

The Jews reported to the commandant the following day and were segregated and sent to a separate barracks. They were told they were being sent to a "newer and better" camp. Approximately 150 to 200 Jewish soldiers had been identified, but the Germans needed 350 to fill a quota, so they also rounded up non-Jews considered "troublemakers" and others who they thought looked Jewish, had Jewish-sounding names, or were circumcised.

The group was then sent on a five-day trip to Berga, a slave-labor camp on the River Elster near the border of Czechoslovakia. Conditions on the train were not unlike those on trains of European Jews deported to concentration camps. The POWs were packed 60 to a boxcar, with a bucket for a toilet. The only food available was what they had smuggled aboard. During the trip, Allied planes strafed and bombed the trains, hitting one of the cars and killing some of the passengers.

When they arrived at Berga, the Jewish prisoners were housed in a foul-smelling, lice-infested barracks that was no more than 35 by 25 feet. It was impossible to see out because bunks blocked the two windows. No heavy blankets or clothing was issued to protect the men from the winter cold, and the one daily meal consisted of a bowl of hot soup and an occasional piece of bread.

"You had to be paired up with another man," said Steckler. "You kept each other warm at night by huddling together. We maintained each other's welfare by sharing body heat, by sharing the paper-thin blankets that were given to us, by sharing the soup, by sharing the bread, by sharing everything."

The men arrived at 1:00 P.M., and half were sent out to work until 6:00; they did not return until 11:00. When they returned, they were covered with white rock dust from hewing an underground chamber to make a synthetic rubber factory out of reach of Allied bombs. They worked with jackhammers, to which "they hitched us up like horses," Steckler recalled. Sometimes a prisoner would not be strong enough to control the jackhammer, and two or three men would have to dig their heels into the ground and stand back to enable them to operate the machine.

When someone paused for a rest, a civilian German overseer would slash at him with a pick or throw a rock at him. Military foremen used rubber hoses to beat prisoners. Steckler paused once and was hit on the hand with a pickax by a civilian. He bandaged the wound with some paper and kept working. Two days later, he paused to adjust the bandage and was knocked unconscious by an overseer who hit him in the head with a shovel. To revive him, the Nazi stomped on Steckler's injured thumb, leaving him with the mangled finger he has today. Prisoners were forced to endure such treatment from sunrise to sunset seven days a week.

One myth about the Holocaust is that Jews went to their deaths like sheep to slaughter. In fact, there were many instances of resistance, but the sad truth was that the Jews in most of the concentration camps were helpless against their captors. Even soldiers, like those sent to Berga, were unable to put up much of a fight against their guards. The labor they were forced to do reduced many to the point that they could hardly walk, let alone resist. Four men once tried to escape, but they were caught and shot. The Germans brought their bodies back to the camp to show the other prisoners what would happen if anyone else tried to escape.

The death of a prisoner provided a reprieve for the others since those who were selected for the burial detail were spared a few hours of work. The survivors would take the dead man into town, where the casket maker would build a wooden coffin. In the meantime, the POWs would beg for food and cigarettes from the townspeople. The coffin would then be buried outside the camp in a civilian cemetery.

When they changed shifts, the prisoners would pass civilians who would tell them what was taking place at Buchenwald. One survivor recalled hearing screams from an area that he later was told was used to skin people alive. Berga was used as a punishment camp where the inmates of Buchenwald could be worked to death. Although no Americans were "exterminated" at Berga, at least 70 POWs died of the effects of slave labor and starvation between February 28, 1945, and the liberation of the camp on April 20, 1945. Ray Weiss reported in an article on May 1, 1983, in the Fort Myers, Florida, *News Press* that no more than 90 to 125 Americans survived the three-months ordeal.

"When we got to the hospital in Paris," Steckler says in "P.O.W.," "I weighed less than 85 pounds. We were lice-ridden, millions of lice in my hair, all over my body. I was shaved from head to foot, except for my moustache, my eyebrows, my eyelids. I was shaved completely. We looked so bad that the nurses, the French nurses' aides used to cry when they came to our bedside. Ran from the bed sometimes. We were in such bad shape that they fed us vitamins, intravenously. And then finally within a few days, we were told we were gonna be shipped back to the States by airplanes because there wasn't much more they could do for us and they were afraid that they weren't doing enough and it might not be possible to save us. If we were to die, we were going to die home."

The survivors located by Weiss had differing opinions as to why they were singled out to be mistreated. Some said that Hitler had ordered Jewish POWs to be removed from all camps, but that the commandant at Berga was the only one who carried out the order. Others told him that the commandant was anti-Semitic and made the decision independently.

One remarkable aspect of this story is that very few people have ever heard it. It is also astonishing that it is not mentioned anywhere in the 42 volumes of documents and testimony presented at the Nuremberg trials, even though mistreatment of POWs was included among the charges brought by the Allies.

For reasons not entirely clear, the United States did not wish to raise the issue of mistreatment of American Jewish soldiers, although Secretary of State Cordell Hull had said in 1944 that his department was "exercising special vigilance to prevent discrimination by German authorities against American prisoners of war upon racial or religious basis." At the time of his statement, Hull claimed no evidence of discrimination, but even after the government received information about mistreatment, apparently no action was taken. It may have been that the government did not want the public to know that American Jewish soldiers had been victims of the Nazis and that the government had done no more to save them than to save the Jews of Europe.

As is true of the Holocaust in general, many claim ignorance. But the truth is that returning soldiers did report mistreatment, including the story of the Berga slave-labor camp. For example, on February 2, 1945, the *New York Times* reported that American POWs were forced to work in slate mines at Bad Orb and that "Jews were segregated and shackled and made to do whatever the Germans desired."

It did not mention, however, that Jewish POWs were sent to Berga. On February 20, two former prisoners at Stalag 2B told the *Times* that American Jewish POWs had been singled out for kickings and cuffings and blows by rifle butt. Daniel Steckler told his story to the *Times* on June 13, 1945, but it went unnoticed for 40 years.

Until now, American Jews have not even been recognized as being among the victims of the Holocaust. The number of American Jews who died is undoubtedly small, but that does not excuse the U.S. government from the obligation it had to defend them while in captivity and, later, to prosecute their murderers. Jews constantly assert the importance of remembering the Holocaust so that it can be prevented from ever happening again. We cannot forget, however, what we never knew.

REFERENCES

Barker, A. J. *Behind Barbed Wire*. London: Batsford, 1974.

Berben, Paul. *Dachau*. London: Norfolk Press, 1975.

Foy, David. *For You the War Is Over*. New York: Stein and Day, 1984.

Gilbert, Martin. *Atlas of the Holocaust*. New York: Macmillan, 1982.

Kowaslki, Issac. *Anthology on Armed Jewish Resistance, 1939–1945*, vol. 1. New York: Jewish Combatants Publishing House, 1984.

Le Chene, Evelyn. *Mauthausen*. London: Methuen, 1971.

Lengyel, Olga. *Five Chimneys*. New York: Howard Fertig, 1983.

Spanjaard, Barry. *Don't Fence Me In*. Santa Clarita, Calif.: B & B, 1981.

Vietor, John. *Time Out*. New York: Richard R. Smith, 1951.

Weinstock, Eugene. *Beyond the Last Path*. New York: Bonnie and Goer, 1947.

Appendix E: American Prisoners of War in World War I, World War II, Korea, and Vietnam: Statistical Data Concerning Numbers Captured, Repatriated, and Still Alive as of January 1, 1992

Charles A. Stenger

Data for this section were developed in cooperation with the Department of Defense, National Research Council, National Archives, and other sources. As such, the section reflects agreement as to the accuracy and acceptability of the information presented. It was prepared for the Veterans Administration Advisory Committee on Former Prisoners of War. Inquiries or comments should be directed to Dr. Charles A. Stenger, American Ex-Prisoners of War Association, 7425 Democracy Boulevard, Bethesda, Maryland, 20817, (301) 365–5452.

ALL WARS

	Total	WWI	WWII	Korean	Vietnam	Persian Gulf
Captured and Interned	142,250	4,120	130,201	7,140	766	23
Still Classified as POW	1	-----	-----	-----	1	-----
Died While POW	17,212	147	14,072	2,701	292	-----
Refused Repatriation	21	-----	-----	21	-----	-----
Returned to U.S. Military Control	125,201	3,973	116,129	4,418	658	23
Alive on January 1, 1982	93,029	633	87,996	3,770	630	-----
Alive on January 1, 1992	68,887	110	65,001	3,155	598	23

Notes: 1. January 1, 1982, data are provided because they most clearly approximate the POW population at the time P.L. 97-37 went into effect (October 1, 1981). As of January 1, 1992, the POW population has decreased through death by 24,068 (26%).

2. While not appropriate for inclusion in POW statistics, 92,584 servicemen were lost in combat and never recovered, as follows: World War I: 3,350; World War II: 78,773; Korea: 8,177; Vietnam: 2,271; Persian Gulf: 13.

3. Data for World War II do not include U.S. merchant marine casualties: 4,780 missing, 882 dead (including 37 POWs), 572 released POWs, and one POW unaccounted for (*Summary of Merchant Marine Casualties, WWII*, July 1, 1950, report of U.S. Coast Guard).

4. World War II data do not include construction workers and Pan American employees (from Guam) on Wake Island who, as a class, were deemed to be veterans for VA purposes in accordance with DOD Directive 1000.20 (PL 95-202). Originally, there were 1,146 of the former and 69 of the latter. An estimated 600 were evacuated. Approximately 600 in all may have been captured. An unofficial estimate of survivors until January 1, 1992, would be 225.

5. During the Civil War, 220,000 (Southern soldiers) were captured by the North, with 26,436 dying during confinement; 126,950 Northern soldiers were captured by the South, with 22,576 dying during confinement (*The Civil War*, New York: Garden Press). During the American Revolution, unofficial reports indicate up to 11,000 died during captivity, most while confined in prison ships in New York Harbor.

WORLD WAR II: TOTAL ARMY, AIR CORPS, NAVY AND MARINES

TOTAL

Captured and Interned	130,201
Died While POW	14,072
Returned to U.S. Military Control	116,129
Alive on January 1, 1982	87,996
Alive on January 1, 1992	65,001

Army and Air Corps

	Total	ETO/Mediat. [a]	Pacific	Other	b/c Philippine Is. (Dec 7, 1941, thru May 10, 1942
Captured & Interned	124,079	93,941	27,465	2,673	(25,580)
Died While POW	12,653	1,121	11,107	425	(10,650)
Returned to U.S. Military Control	111,426	92,820	16,358	2,248	(14,930)
Alive on Jan 1, 1982	84,753	71,736	11,280	1,737	(10,295)
Alive on Jan 1, 1992	62,693	53,368	8,045	1,280	(7,320)

[a] Includes 23,554 captured during the Battle of Bulge (Ardennes, Dec. 16, 1944, to Jan. 25, 1945).

[b] Also known as the Bataan-Corregidor combat zone. Statistics in this column are incorporated in the Pacific totals.

[c] U.S. forces captured included approximately 17,000 American nationals and 12,000 Filipino Scouts. During the first year of captivity, a reported 30% of the Americans and 80% of the Filipino Scouts died. Data are unclear as to the proportion of each group surviving to repatriation, but a very rough estimate would be 11,000 Americans and 4,000 Filipino Scouts. This information is based on military records developed during the war, and no accurate breakdown was made after repatriation. In addition, some 7,300 American civilian men, women, and children were involuntarily incarcerated by the Japanese in 1941–1942. Approximately 3,706 are alive as of January 1, 1992. An additional 13,000 Amerasians holding American citizenship hid out during the period and were never interned; of these, 2,900 are estimated to be alive as of January, 1, 1992.

Navy & Marine Corps

	Total	Navy [a]	Marine Corps [b]
Captured & Interned	6,122	3,848	2,274
Died While POW	1,419	901	518
Returned to U.S. Military Control	4,703	2,947	1,756
Alive on Jan 1, 1982	3,243	2,032	1,211
Alive on Jan 1, 1992	2,308	1,443	865

[a] Navy casualty data related to naval vessels, not to theater of operation.

[b] Marine Corps personnel captured in Philippine Islands between December 1941 and May 1942 totaled 1,388. Data on the number of Marines who died during captivity, were repatriated, or are still living are not available for this theater of operations.

KOREAN CONFLICT[a/b]

	Total	Army	Navy	Marine	Air Force
Captured & Interned	7,140	6,656	35	225	224
Died While POW	2,701	2,662	4	31	4
Returned to U.S. Military Control	4,418	3,973	31	194	220
Refused Repatriation	21	21	--	---	---
Alive on Jan 1, 1982	3,770	3,390	26	166	188
Alive on Jan 1, 1992	3,155	2,837	19	141	158

[a] These data indicate status through November 4, 1954. As of that date, 24 were still missing. By September 15, 1955, 15 of these men had been released and the other nine were declared dead.

[b] Does not include 81 Navy personnel who were involved in the Pueblo incident.

VIETNAM

Returned Alive		Remains Returned		Still MIA	
USAF	333	USAF	174	USAF	822
US Navy	151	US Navy	87	US Navy	448
US Army	136	US Army	35	US Army	675
US Marines	38	US Marines	14	US Marines	283
		Service not		US Coast Guard	1
		identified	2	Civilians	42
Totals:	658		312		2,271

Notes: 1. These are the latest data from the National League of Families of American Prisoners of War and MIAs in Southeast Asia. Approximately 771 were captured and 113 of them were designated by DoD as dying in captivity. The total escaping or surviving to repatriation is 658.

2. One American serviceman is still officially designated as POW. This is a symbolic classification, given because the U.S. Government cannot prove beyond doubt that no American remains alive. It is estimated that 598 of the original 658 remain alive as of January 1, 1992.

PERSIAN GULF

The total number of American servicemen captured by Iraq was 23; all were repatriated immediately when hostilities ceased. Originally, an additional 26 were listed as MIAs, but bodies of 13 were recovered. The other 13 are presumed to have been lost over water, although their status remains unknown.

SOURCES

World War II

1. Department of Defense. *Army Battle Casualties and Non-Battle Deaths in WWII*. Final Report, Dec. 7, 1941 to Dec. 31, 1946. Washington, D.C.: GPO, June 1, 1953.

2. Department of Defense. *Combat Connected Naval Casualties*. World War II by states—1946. UNS-MC-CG, 2 vols. Washington, D.C.: Casualty Section, Navy Department, 1946.

3. Department of Defense. *History of Medical Department of Navy in WWII: Statistics of Diseases and Injuries*. Washington, D.C.: GPO (Navy Med. p. 1318, vol. 3), 1950.

4. Department of Defense. *History of U.S. Marine Corps Operations in WWII*, vol. 5, Appendix A. Washington, D.C.: Historical Branch, G-3 Division, Headquarters, U.S. Marine Corps, 1968.

Korean War

1. Department of Defense. Public Information Release no. 1088–54. Washington, D.C.: Office of Secretary of Defense, Nov. 5, 1954.
2. Department of Defense. Tentative Final Report of U.S. Battle Casualties in the Korean War. Washington, D.C.: Office of Secretary of Defense, Nov. 4, 1954.

Vietnam War

1. Data developed by National Archives Machine Readable Division from records provided by the Office of the Secretary of Defense and verified by the POW/MIA Office in the Pentagon.

General

1. Estimates for the number of World War I, World War II, and Korean War prisoners alive on January 1, 1990, are provided by William Page, Medical Follow-up Agency, National Research Council:

For World War I, the number estimated to be still alive on January 1, 1990, is based on U.S. life tables for white males, 1969–71, and on the assumption that they were living on January 1, 1991, at the rate predicted by the NRC study of World War I veterans in 1960.

For World War II prisoners, the number estimated to be alive on January 1, 1990, is based on a recent study of mortality of POWs to January 1, 1976. (Robert J. Keehan, Follow-up Studies of World War II and Korean Conflict Prisoners: III Mortality to January 1, 1976, *American Journal of Epidemiology*, February 1980), and the application of 1978 U.S. death rates updated to January 1, 1990.

For Korean War prisoners, survival data for January 1, 1990, is based on a sample of Korean POWs in the *American Journal of Epidemiology* mortality study and the application of the same 1978 U.S. death rate tables as above.

Bibliography

Arthur, Arnold. *Deliverance at Los Banos*. New York: St. Martin's Press, 1985.

Knox, Donald. *Death March: The Survivors of Bataan*. New York: Harcourt Brace Jovanovich, 1981.

Lawton, Marion R. *Some Survived: An Epic Account of Japanese Captivity During World War II*. Chapel Hill, N.C.: Algonquin Books, 1984.

Schultz, Duane. *Hero of Bataan: The Story of Jonathan M. Wainwright*. New York: St. Martin's Books, 1981.

Spector, Ronald H. *Eagle Against The Sun: The American War With Japan*. New York: The Free Press, 1985.

Index

Vietnam War, words of an American captured during, xvi

Wainwright, General Jonathan M., 6, 25, 27
Walters, Bucky, 64, 65

Weiss, Paul, definition of idiocide, xvii
Witting, John, experiment with laboratory rats, xviii–xix

Zempke, Colonel, 91

ABOUT THE AUTHOR

TOM BIRD co-wrote *Willie Stargell: An Autobiography* and *Knuckleballs* with Phil Niekro. His work has also appeared in many magazines.